Writing
TO
STANDARDS

KATHY KIRK

Writing
TO
STANDARDS

Teacher's Resource of
Writing Activities for PreK-6

CORWIN PRESS, INC.
A Sage Publications Company
Thousand Oaks, California

For information:

Corwin Press, Inc.
A Sage Publications Company
2455 Teller Road
Thousand Oaks, California 91320
E-mail: order@corwinpress.com

Sage Publications Ltd.
6 Bonhill Street
London EC2A 4PU
United Kingdom

Sage Publications India Pvt. Ltd.
M-32 Market
Greater Kailash I
New Delhi 110 048 India

Printed in the United States of America

Library of Congress Cataloging-in-Publication Data

Kirk, Kathy.
    Writing to standards: Teacher's resource of writing activities for
pre-K-6/ by Kathy Kirk.
        p. cm.
    Includes bibliographical references and index.
        ISBN 0-7619-7638-8 (cloth : alk. paper) — ISBN 0-7619-7639-6 (pbk.: alk. paper)
        1. English language—Composition and exercises—Study and teaching
(Elementary) —Activity programs—United States. 2. English language—
Study and teaching (Elementary) —Standards—United States. I. Title.
    LB1576.K49 2000
    372.62'3044—dc21   00-009024

This book is printed on acid-free paper.

01 02 03 04 05 06 07 7 6 5 4 3 2 1

Corwin Editorial Assistant: Julia Parnell
Production Editor: Diane S. Foster
Editorial Assistant: Victoria Cheng
Typesetter/Designer: Tina Hill
Cover Designer: Oscar Desierto

Contents

Acknowledgments

I run the risk of forgetting to thank someone for his or her help and inspiration in writing this workbook, but I truly appreciate the support that I have received. The following people stand foremost in my mind:

Thank you to my husband, John, and my children, Sarah, Kaitlin, and Matthew Kirk. Not only have they been patient with all my hours at the computer, but also they sacrifice their privacy by allowing me to write about them in my newspaper column and to share parts of those columns here.

Nanci Schneider, Salem-Keizer School District Administrator, planted the seed for this project when I was volunteering in Matthew's classroom. Thank you, Nanci, for believing in my writing abilities and encouraging me to pursue my goals.

Sara Swanberg, coordinator of the Arts in Education (AIE) program of the Salem Art Association, sprinkled water on the seed when she hired me to participate in AIE. She offered invaluable suggestions and made it a joy to be a part of the program.

Nancy Fisher, Karen Stai, Nancy Russell, Dixie Moravec, Barbara Leisman, and Teri Johnston, classroom teachers, took time out of their busy schedules to review drafts of this manuscript. They offered words of support and wonderful suggestions for changes.

Joni Gilles, former teacher and principal at the Howard Street Charter School, set the perfect example of "following your dreams" and pushed me toward mine. Thank you, Joni, from the bottom of my heart.

There are too many other teachers and students with whom I have volunteered and worked during the last 12 years to name them all individually. But you all know who you are, and I thank you for the many things that you have taught me about the joy of writing.

About the Author

Kathy Kirk used professional writing skills in a variety of employment settings as a registered nurse for 15 years. As a volunteer, she has taught writing in elementary classrooms since 1988. A freelance writer and writing instructor since 1998, she contributes a regular column and feature articles to the *Keizertimes* (Keizer, Oregon) newspaper and feature articles to the *Statesman Journal* (Salem, Oregon) newspaper. She has contributed articles to the *American Journal of Nursing* and a local parent newsletter. Previously, she conducted a writer's workshop for first- through fifth-grade students through the Artist-in-Residence program sponsored by the Salem Oregon Art Association and taught a journalism class for middle school students at Howard Street Charter School in Salem, Oregon. Since 1998, she has worked as a freelance writer contributing a regular column and feature articles to two Oregon newspapers and a parent newsletter. Her work has also appeared in the *American Journal of Nursing,* and she writes copy as a marketing assistant.

CORWIN
PRESS

The Corwin Press logo—a raven striding across an open book—represents the happy union of courage and learning. We are a professional-level publisher of books and journals for K–12 educators, and we are committed to creating and providing resources that embody these qualities. Corwin's motto is "Success for All Learners."

Introduction

Every child is unique with a history of individual experiences. Each child has a fresh perspective of the world. Almost all children have a zest for life that includes the curiosity to learn and develop new skills. The majority of children have the ability to be natural and gifted storytellers.

Because I believe each of the statements above, and because my nontraditional teaching experiences in kindergarten through eighth grade have been so rewarding, I eagerly accepted the challenge to develop this workbook.

I used my successes, both in the classroom and as a professional writer, for a springboard to develop the writing activities. I also researched state educational writing standards and reform. My intent is to help elementary students master the writing traits that educators have agreed are fundamental. Although the activities cannot possibly cover all aspects of writing, they do provide an excellent introduction to essential writing traits. They also focus students to view writing as a process and not just as a finished product.

The workbook is divided into chapters that highlight one of the following writing traits: voice, ideas and content, word choice, sentence fluency, organization, and conventions. Each chapter begins with a question and an answer. The writing activities and writing samples that follow give students a hands-on opportunity to explore the writing trait. After students have been exposed to the techniques that real-world writers use, they will be able to effectively produce writing that is purposeful and clear.

My experience as a freelance journalist encouraged me to bring newspaper writing into the classroom and into this workbook. Students of all ages respond well to the novelty of journalism, and the community paper is an excellent resource for engaging students in the writing process. Some of the exercises in this workbook incorporate the use of newspapers as a teaching resource.

I designed the activities for students with a wide range of writing abilities. The activities can be used as whole-class exercises or can be worked independently by individual students. Activities fit into current classroom curriculum. Last, but not least, I tried to incorporate my love of written language so that students can experience a sense of joy and have fun as they learn the how-tos of written communication.

1

Voice

Who am I when I write?

Voice is telling the reader:

- This is who I am.
- This is me in the form of writing.

I may write about the same facts that another writer uses, but my writing will sound like me because of the particular descriptions and details that only I can provide.

I put my personality into my writing by including things important to me, such as

- My family and memories
- My opinions and beliefs
- My traditions, hobbies, and habits
- My understanding of the way the world works
- My style of using words and language when I speak out loud

When I write, I think about my reader:

- I try to imagine questions the reader may ask. I use my voice to answer those questions. I may also ask questions to make my reader think about what I've written.

- I use a clear writing voice so that it is easy for my reader to understand what I mean.

Just as I talk differently with different people, I can change my writing voice:

- I use a familiar, everyday voice with family and a more formal voice with strangers.

- I choose words to communicate my mood; I can write in a serious or a funny voice.

- I choose to use my voice in the best writing style that communicates my message.

Illustrating Voice With Pictures

Draw two to three pictures. These pictures will stand for your writing voice. Draw things you like to do, memories you have, people in your family, or anything that tells about you. You may also write a word or two by each picture to tell more about yourself.

Examining Invitations to Explore Voice

Look at the pictures below. Pretend that you are going to have a party or a special event. Draw a circle around two guests who would enjoy this party. On another paper, draw an invitation or use your writing voice to invite each guest.

For example, you might use your writing voice in a humorous way to invite your friend the fish to a swimming party. You could write, "Please, glub, glub, come to a pool party, glub, glub, at my house on Saturday from 4 to 8 p.m. We will have, glub, glub, wormy refreshments." (You could draw bubbles on your invitation and use the words "glub, glub" to pretend that you were underwater inviting the fish to the party.)

Creating Invitations to Explore Voice

Pretend that you are planning a celebration. What questions will your guests have? What information must you provide? In the space below or on another paper, use your writing voice to create an invitation. Include all the necessary information. Here are some hints:

- What kind of event are you planning?

- Would you write the same words for a graduation invitation as for a Halloween party?

- Is it a "just drop by" or a "come at a special time" event? What details do your guests need to know (such as date, time, address, directions, and things to bring)?

- Choose descriptive words that will make guests excited to come and that will make them think, "This is just the kind of party I would expect from you!"

Focusing on Personal Characteristics

If you share things about yourself, you make your writing special in a way that no one else can. This is called *writing in your own voice.* List five words or phrases to describe your personality. Choose words that describe specific information about you and how your writing voice is shaped. Choose words that show you are really "a unique individual!" (For an example, look at the words in the box below.)

To describe herself, one author used the following words: (1) family-centered, (2) curious, (3) quirky or unusual sense of humor, and (4) conscientious. She reminded people that (5) "dynamite comes in small packages!"

Read the statements below. They tell you things that shape this author's writing voice. Choose a number from the personality traits in the box and match it with the correct statement below. The first one is done for you.

<u> 4 </u> The author tries to be on time for appointments, and she does what she knows is right.

_____ The author loves to read books. Books have introduced the author to many new ideas.

_____ The author's children are her favorite people. She likes to do things with them.

_____ The author likes to cook. She joked, "I wonder how to make jelly-bean-stuffed ants."

_____ Being short doesn't keep the author from having big dreams.

Expressing Voice by Sharing Details

When you share your opinions, your observations (the things you see), and your thoughts, you are expressing your voice. When you write, include

- Things about your family, your feelings, and facts about the things you know and like

- Details to show readers your understanding of the world around you

Read the two selections below. Both were written about a dog named Tyler. Which example is boring and sounds like any dog? Which selection has a voice that describes Tyler in a unique way so that you can picture her?

1. I have a dog. My dog's name is Tyler. Tyler likes me. Tyler likes to run and play. I like my dog, and I like to play with my dog. My dog likes people. Tyler likes to be in my backyard.

My dog is a black dog. Sometimes she barks, but sometimes she is quiet. She likes to eat. She mostly eats dog food, but sometimes I give her dog biscuits. Usually, she eats the same kind of dog food, but sometimes I buy a different kind. Whatever I give her, she will eat it. People think my dog is nice. Do you think my dog is nice?

2. My dog is a girl dog, but you might not know it when you hear her name. We got "Tyler" when she was 15 months old. The lady that gave her to us said, "I always wanted to name a little girl Tyler, so that's what I named the dog." My children think this is funny because they think Tyler sounds more like a boy's name than a girl's name.

Tyler is a black Labrador, and she is true to her breed—she is friendly and likes people. If I go into my backyard to do anything, Tyler comes over and leans her body against my leg just so she can touch me and be close to me. It's also her way of saying, "I want some attention!"

Sometimes, Tyler does silly things to get attention. She might flop on her back with a chew toy in her mouth and peddle her legs in the air. She'll give me a look that says, "Aren't I being goofy right now?" Other times, she runs in large circles around the yard just as if she is running on a racetrack and trying to take first place. She'll go around and around, faster and faster, until I finally say, "OK, Tyler, I see what you're doing, so quit showing off and stop!"

Write a paragraph or two about your own pet or a family member. Use your unique voice by including specific details that help readers see things from your point of view.

Controlling Voice to Fit the Reading Audience

Use another sheet of paper to write a letter to a family member or a close friend.

1. Write a greeting to start your letter.

2. Write a few sentences about something that happened to you this week or include something you learned. Provide details. Think of questions that your reader might ask, and try to answer those questions.

3. Use a few sentences to describe your feelings. Use words that fit with the feelings.

4. Write the words that will serve as a closing to your letter.

Would your reader know that you wrote this letter even if you didn't sign your name? If the answer is yes, then you have done a good job of "writing in your own voice."

Answer the following questions:

It's customary to use words such as *hi* and *with love* in letters to people that you know well, but you don't write this way to strangers or in business letters. Look for the letters to the editor in a newspaper. What words did people use before signing their names? If you wrote a letter to the paper, you would probably change your writing voice from your first letter. You would end your newspaper letter with a word such as *sincerely*.

If you write to your best friend to share your opinion about the cafeteria food, you don't have to name your school. But if you write a letter about cafeteria food to the newspaper, the school name is an important detail to include. Do you see how you can change your writing voice and provide different details depending on how well you know your reader?

Exploring Characters in Literature to Express Voice

Sometimes, authors use fictional characters to create the voice of a story. Read each selection below. Match them with the fictional characters that follow. Think about how the authors used their writing voices to create characters that stand out for readers.

1. "Only the micies know that," he said. "Spiders is also talking a great deal. You might not be thinking it but spiders is the most tremendous natterboxes. And when they is spinning their webs, they is singing all the time. They is singing sweeter than a nightengull."

2. There were two cupcakes in Philip Parker's lunch bag and Albert got a Hershey bar with almonds and Paul's mother gave him a piece of jelly roll that had little coconut sprinkles on top. Guess who's mother forgot to put in dessert?

3. "Sorry, Sorry, Sorry. I'm sitting-sitting on my eggs. Eight of them. Got to keep them toasty-oasty warm. I have to stay right here, I'm no flibberty-ibberty-gibbert. I do not play when there are eggs to hatch. I'm expecting goslings."

4. "Alice is somebody that nobody can see," said Frances. "And that is why she does not have a birthday. So I'm singing Happy Thursday to her."
   "Today is Friday," said Mother.
   "It is Thursday for Alice," said Frances.
   "Alice will not have h-r-n-d, and she will not have g-k-l-s. But we are singing together."
   "What are h-r-n-d and g-k-l-s?" asked Mother.
   "Cake and candy. I thought you could spell," said Frances.

_____ Alexander from *Alexander and the Terrible, Horrible, No Good, Very Bad Day* by Judith Viorst (The author uses run-on sentences and lots of details to make her point.)

_____ The Big Friendly Giant from *The BFG* by Roald Dahl (The author creates a unique voice by making up words that closely resemble real words and by using improper English. In the book, the author explains that the main character speaks this way because he has never been to school.)

_____ Frances from *A Birthday for Frances* by Russell Hoban (This author often has the main character recite poetry or sing songs in the story to show what she likes and thinks. The author creates a humorous voice by giving readers a picture of the world through the opinionated eyes of the young character.)

_____ The goose from *Charlotte's Web* by E. B. White (This author uses repetition of words and made-up rhyming phrases and sentences to create a character with a lively and original voice.)

Note to the teacher: You may want to read other passages from these books to your students. Don't identify the book, but see if the students can distinguish the characters. Have students name the specific traits in the passage that provided clues to the identity of the character and the author's voice.

Searching for Voice in Newspaper Comics

You can find examples of the way authors use their writing voice in newspaper comics. Cartoonists have the advantage of using both drawings and written words to communicate their message. Not all comics are written just to be funny. Authors of comic strips may use their voice to do the following:

- Provide humor and make you laugh

- Bring a serious message about politics (government) or culture (the way people live)

- Give useful information to readers

Look in a newspaper and try to find the following comic strips. Then answer the questions about each cartoonist's writing voice.

"The Family Circus" by Bil Keane: Mr. Keane uses his writing voice to create a world in which we see things through the eyes of the children who are main characters in this comic strip. Do you think that some of the things the children say would sound as funny if grown-ups were speaking these lines? Why did you say "yes" or "no"?

"Baby Blues" by Rick Kirkman and Jerry Scott: In "The Family Circus," the children have always remained the same age, but Zoe in "Baby Blues" started as a toddler and has grown older in the comic strip. The cartoonists also added a baby brother to the family. As the family grows and changes, the cartoonists can use their voice in different ways. For example, they can write about different topics as the children's interests change.

As the family ages and changes, would the authors need to use different word choices to express their writing voice? Give an example. (Think about the way a 2-year-old talks and the way a teenager talks.)

Search for comic strips that have the following voices. Write the name of the comic strip below the comic strip description.

A comic strip that uses an animal as a main character voice

A comic strip that makes jokes about the way our government is run (You may need to look on the editorial page in the newspaper, rather than in the comic section.)

A comic strip that has a continuous story that runs day after day (This is like a television show with a plot that you follow from one episode to the next.)

On another paper, you may express your humorous voice by drawing a comic strip and writing in words of your own.

Choosing Words to Express Voice

When you write, you can choose words that affect your writing voice. You can select

- Words that communicate a variety of feelings and emotions
- Special expressions that communicate extra meaning to readers
- Specific details that put your personality or viewpoint into your writing

The following paragraphs are from a newspaper column about schoolteachers. Read the paragraphs. Look for examples of word choice that help create the voice of this writing.

When Kaitlin went to school, her teachers showed they valued her sense of excitement and her sense of humor. Her teachers knew that Kaitlin had the same red hair as her older sister, but they treated her like a unique individual.

At times, Kaitlin's mother struggled. She thought, "What are the values of my child's village? How will Kaitlin learn these things?"

Kaitlin's teacher, Mrs. Guitierrez, and a rabbit named Trixie taught Kaitlin about independence and interdependence. Kaitlin developed a kind and caring attitude because her teachers treated all of the students this way.

The author provides details about teachers. Underline one of these details. Does this detail say something good or bad about teachers?

Is the writer's viewpoint funny or serious? (Did the writer want to make you laugh or to tell you something serious?)

What did the writer mean by, "Trixie taught Kaitlin about independence and interdependence"? The writer could have said, "There was a rabbit in the classroom. The rabbit showed Kaitlin that sometimes she needed to work alone and sometimes she needed to get help by working in a group." Which word choice sounds more interesting?

You may have heard the expression, "It takes a whole village to raise a child." Who is the author talking about when she wrote, "What are the values of my child's village?"

The author shared personal information about her family to create a unique voice. The author chose specific words to describe Kaitlin and her teachers. What did you learn about Kaitlin's appearance and personality? What did you learn about her teachers?

On another sheet of paper, write a paragraph or two about one of your teachers, a family member, or a friend. Watch your word choice! Use your voice to

- Provide details (Help readers see this person's appearance and personality.)

- Create the mood (The reader should be able to tell if it is happy, angry, sad, etc.)

- Include special words or expressions that help readers picture this person

Changing Voice by Using Different Writing Methods

When you speak language out loud, you can change the way you talk. You think about the person to whom you are speaking. You may use a loud or a soft voice. You talk louder to a person who cannot hear well. You can show emotions by changing the sound of your voice. You may raise the pitch of your voice to show that you are excited.

You can change your writing voice by using different methods or writing modes. Below are examples of some writing modes.

1. Expository: The writer explains information or teaches how to do something. The writer must know the topic, provide details, be creative, and explain the information in a clear way. A cooking column that provides recipes and how-to tips about preparing food is an example of expository writing.

2. Narrative: The writer tells a story. The writer must grab the reader's attention with the first line of writing. The writer introduces readers to the characters and setting, states a problem, gives two or three events that lead to a solution, and describes how the problem was resolved. Astronaut Jim Lovell wrote a narrative story about the problems he experienced aboard the spacecraft *Apollo 13.*

3. Descriptive: The writer paints a picture with words. The writer chooses interesting and specific details about the topic. The writer presents a clear and sharp picture by describing the way things look and by including sounds, smells, feelings, and touch. You could use descriptive writing to report on a trip to Disneyland.

4. Imaginative: The writer uses her voice to create "make-believe" or something that is not real. The writer creates a new idea or a new way to make readers think. The writer provides unusual details and surprises that no one else would think of writing. Author J. K. Rowling used imaginative writing in creating her series of books about wizard Harry Potter.

5. Persuasive: The writer tries to convince readers to see things from his view or to change how readers think. The writer first states a problem and then provides a personal opinion supported by clear facts, information, and sensible thinking. The writer may suggest a plan of action. Opinion articles and editorial columns in newspapers provide examples of persuasive writing.

Choose the best method for a newspaper reporter to use her writing voice for the assignments below. Place the number of an appropriate writing mode next to each.

_____ An article that describes the exhibits students saw at a science museum

_____ A column that gives an opinion about chewing gum in school

_____ An article that explains how to play a popular computer game

_____ An eyewitness account from the person who rescued a drowning dog

_____ A pretend report about Martians arriving in your town for a Halloween celebration

On another paper, use your writing voice to tell an imaginative story. Include unusual details.

2

Ideas and Content

What do I want to say when I write? What is the purpose of my writing?

- I must choose a topic—the main idea.

- If I choose topics that have meaning to me and if I share my feelings and opinions, I will communicate more powerfully.

- I must clearly communicate my main idea with details. I help readers understand what I mean when I provide specific details.

- I can use my memory and all my senses, as well as factual information, to provide details.

- I must focus my writing so that I include only purposeful details. I eliminate details that do not fit with my topic.

- I must choose a writing style (or mode). I think about the audience that I am writing for and the message that I want to communicate when I select an appropriate writing style.

If I write well, readers will say, "The author clearly communicated her idea and provided details that were interesting."

Sorting Pictures to Focus on Details

Look at the groups of pictures below. Cross out the picture that you would not include in each group. Think of a story that you could tell with the remaining pictures. Tell that story to a classmate or write it on another piece of paper.

Using Drawings to Examine Details

Pretend your main idea is about feelings. Look at the details in the faces below. Write words for the feelings that you see. Name the details in the face that made you think of that feeling. The first picture is done for you. Then, on another piece of paper, draw one face or picture with details that show feelings. Write descriptive words by your drawing to name the feeling.

Anger or Rage

I see slits drawn to represent eyes shut tight, wrinkles in the forehead, and lines showing the mouth turned down at the corners. I think people look like this when they are so angry that they scrunch their face up and grit their teeth.

Creating Drawings to Focus on Main Ideas

In the boxes below, draw pictures. Each box should represent one main idea, and the details in your picture should be about that main idea. Write words for your main idea. (For example: If the main idea is "favorite sports," you can draw pictures of a soccer ball, a football field, or other things that have to do with sports. But you would have to put pictures of your "favorite foods" in a different box for a different main idea.)

Main   Idea:

Main   Idea:

Identifying Main Ideas and Matching Details

The main idea is feelings. List three feelings. Under each feeling, write details that you would use to describe the feeling. Be creative and have fun!

Here is an example:

Anger: blazing eyes, snarling mouth, booming voice, clenched fists, a tornado racing around inside of my belly, a door slamming hard, "Leave me alone, world!"

Feeling #1 _____

Detail words _____

_____

_____

Feeling #2 _____

Detail words _____

_____

_____

Feeling #3 _____

Detail words _____

_____

_____

Brainstorming Details That Match Main Ideas

Below is a list of main ideas. On another piece of paper, write down at least two of the main ideas. Underneath each one, list details that you might use if you were to write about the main idea. Include only information that goes with the main idea you have chosen. (Don't choose the example that is given.)

Main ideas:

Kinds of pets

Types of automobiles

Outdoor activities

Best places to go on vacation

Toys or games that don't require batteries or electricity

Things you might see or do on the Fourth of July

Things you might see in a candy shop

Example: Details for main idea of "Healthy Snacks":

"Ants on a log" (celery with peanut butter and raisins)

Bagel with cream cheese

Homemade applesauce

Fresh pineapple juice

Popcorn sprinkled with herbs

Fresh fruit blended with cottage cheese

Sorting Words to Match Details With Main Ideas

Each list below represents a group of words used in two newspaper articles. Some of the words, at first glance, may not appear to go together. But these words provide the details about the main idea. Read each main idea and the detail words.

Main Idea #1:
The Home Team Wins the Big Game
score
touchdown
school
grandstand
cheering
marching band

Main Idea #2:
A New School Opens in a Community
history books
principal
science
education
goals
students

Now look at the following list of words. Put the number "1" by each word that you could use when writing about Main Idea #1. Put the number "2" by each word that fits with Main Idea #2. Some words may fit both ideas. Cross out any words that you could not use to write about either main idea.

_____ field goal   _____ cows   _____ football
_____ toast   _____ teachers   _____ celebration
_____ computers   _____ saucer   _____ mathematics

Matching Sentences With Main Ideas

When you write about a subject,

- Provide details that clearly belong with your main idea
- Don't include details that are about a different subject—or you will bore or confuse your reader

Below are two main ideas. Following the main ideas are sentences. Match each sentence with one of the main ideas. Write the letter "A" or "B" by each sentence to show which details go with each main idea.

(A) Soccer   (B) Cigarette Smoking

_____ Doctors know this activity damages your lungs.

_____ Shoes with cleats are worn when this activity is done outdoors.

_____ In most states, it is against the law to sell tobacco to people under age 18.

_____ A cartoon character that featured a camel was used in advertisements. This concerned parents because they thought that it would make children want to smoke.

_____ It's OK to use your head, but not your hands, during play (unless you play goalie).

_____ Shin guards are protective equipment worn to prevent leg injuries.

_____ Even being around secondhand smoke can cause health problems for people.

_____ Officials may issue a "yellow, warning card" if a player breaks a rule.

Generating Writing Topics

Have you ever complained, "I don't know what to write about"? To choose a topic,

- Write about memories of a special time in your life
- Think about something that really happened to you
- Choose something about which you have strong feelings (You feel proud, happy, sad, scared, or some other strong emotion.)

Once you choose a topic, talk with a friend to help you remember how you felt and to remember the way things happened, looked, sounded, smelled, and tasted.

Below is a survey to help you choose a writing topic. Answer three of the questions on another paper. Then list three topics about which you could write.

1. List the names of the most important people in your life and their relationship to you.

2. Describe a memory that includes smells.

3. What is the worst thing that someone can do to annoy you?

4. Describe the most unusual place that you have ever visited or would like to go to.

5. If you had to spend a day without electricity, how would you spend your time?

6. Describe 5 minutes in your life that you will never forget.

7. Name your oldest or most prized possession.

8. What is the most unfair thing that has ever happened to you?

9. What are the three words that best describe your personality?

10. Name one thing that you want to change about yourself.

11. What skill or hobby do you have that you could teach someone else?

Focusing Writing Topics

When you choose a main idea, you may have a difficult time providing interesting details if you try to write about too many things at one time. When you choose a main idea, do the following:

- Focus, or zoom in, on a specific part of your main idea. Think about the smaller topics into which your main idea can be divided.

- Choose a smaller topic of the main idea and write about that.

Below are several examples of main ideas and topics. A writer could provide general information about the main idea and more specific details about the focused topics.

Main Idea: *Skateboarding*

Topic #1:	Types of jumps performed by skateboarders
Topic #2:	Ideal clothing and protective gear needed for skateboarding
Topic #3:	Best places to go skateboarding

Main Idea: *A Visit to Grandmother's Farm*

Topic #1:	Gathering eggs from the henhouse
Topic #2:	Learning to make jelly on a wood-burning stove
Topic #3:	Exploring for treasures in Grandma's attic

Main Idea: *Baking*

Topic #1:	How to make an angel food cake
Topic #2:	How to make a perfect piecrust
Topic #3: cookies	Making and decorating Christmas

List three main ideas. Think of a general subject about which to write. (See examples on page 29.)

Main Idea #1 _____

Main Idea #2 _____

Main Idea #3 _____

Now choose two of those main ideas and focus them into three specific topics about which you could provide interesting details. (See examples on page 29.)

Main Idea _____

    Topic #1 _____

    Topic #2 _____

    Topic #3 _____

Main Idea _____

    Topic #1 _____

    Topic #2 _____

    Topic #3 _____

Using Observation to Develop Main Ideas

Sometimes, writers have a hard time thinking of something about which to write. This is called "writer's block." Here are activities that can spark new ideas for writing:

- Watch people and notice events happening around you.

- Read and talk with other people about your observations or opinions.

One writer watched her teenage daughters as they took care of their 4-year-old neighbor, Stephanie. The child liked to play a game in which she gave everyone new names. If anyone forgot the new names and called people by their real names, Stephanie stamped her foot and said, "No, that's not your name!" Stephanie also did many other silly things that made them laugh. The author wrote a funny newspaper column about this event.

Another time, a writer had guests from Japan stay at her house. She learned that people live differently in Japan. Not only do they speak a different language, but also they eat other food, play different games, and have different customs. But as the writer made friends with her guests, she found out that American and Japanese people also have many things in common. The author wrote a newspaper column about what she learned.

Think about the following experiences and talk with another student about the details. Then, on another paper, choose and write about one of these topics:

- Something unusual that you have seen or heard other people talking about

- A time when you learned to do something new or watched a younger child play

- A special place you visited, something interesting you read, or someone you met

Identifying the Best Writing Mode to Communicate Ideas

Once you have decided on a main idea, you need a writing plan. You need to decide the method to present information to readers. Writing methods are also called writing modes. Here are some writing modes:

1. Expository: The writer explains information or teaches how to do something. The writer must know the topic, provide details, be creative, and explain the information in a clear way. You could use expository writing to write about video game equipment.

2. Narrative: The writer tells a story. The writer must grab the reader's attention with the first line of writing. The writer introduces readers to the characters and setting, states a problem, gives two or three events that lead to a solution, and describes how the problem was resolved. You could use narrative writing to write about your experience in a tornado.

3. Descriptive: The writer paints a picture with words. The writer chooses interesting and specific details about the topic. The writer presents a clear and sharp picture by describing the way things look and including sounds, smells, feelings, and touch. You could use descriptive writing to report on the entries in a parade.

4. Imaginative: The writer uses her voice to create "make-believe" or something that is not real. The writer creates a new idea or a new way to make readers think. The writer provides unusual details and surprises that no one else would think of writing. When you write a story that is fiction, you use imaginative writing.

5. Persuasive: The writer tries to convince readers to see things from his point of view or to change how readers think. The writer first states a problem and then provides a personal opinion supported by clear facts, information, and sensible thinking. The writer may suggest a plan of action. You would use persuasive writing to convince your parents to give you an increase in your monthly allowance.

Identify the best writing mode to complete the following writing assignments. (Choose the name of a writing mode from the above list and match it with an assignment.)

A report about the invention of television _____

An article that tries to convince readers to vote _____

An article that describes types of race cars _____

An article that tells about the struggles of a pioneer family _____

A book of tall tales (made-up stories) _____

On another paper, use expository writing to provide information about your town.

1. Decide what questions your report should include (such as what types of work people do, interesting attractions, and how the community was named).

2. Decide where to gather this information and other details.

3. Narrow your topic with a focus.

4. Gather and organize your research.

5. Write a rough draft with interesting details.

Practicing the Persuasive Writing Mode

You use persuasive writing when

- You want to get readers to see things from your point of view
- You want to change the opinion of your readers
- You want to convince readers to think as you do

Planning steps for persuasive writing include the following:

- Decide what your opinion is and how to clearly state what you believe
- Identify three detailed reasons or "pieces of evidence" in favor of your argument
- Think of a way to summarize your facts with a conclusion

Look at the example of a persuasive writing plan in the box below.

Opinion: Cigarette smoking should not be allowed in public buildings.

Reason #1: Scientists' studies show that breathing other people's cigarette smoke can be harmful to the heart and lungs of people who don't smoke.

Reason #2: Cigarette smoke can pollute the clothes and hair of people standing near a smoker. Then people stink like smoke, even if they don't want to smell that way.

Reason #3: People who have allergies and asthma can develop colds more easily if they are forced to breathe cigarette smoke.

Conclusion: People who do not smoke can still be harmed by the cigarette smoke of other people.

On another paper, write a persuasive writing plan to answer this question: "Should students have a school schedule that includes class attendance in summer?" Clearly state your opinion, give three detailed reasons for your opinion, and summarize your conclusion.

Matching Parts of a Newspaper to Content

Newspapers are divided into different sections. Each section is written for a different reason. When readers want to know certain information, they know where to look.

- The "Entertainment" section provides news about fun events and things to do.

- The "Sports" section is written to give readers articles about sports and recreation.

- In the "Travel" section, readers expect to find news about places to take vacations and information needed to travel.

Here is a list of written things that might appear in a newspaper:

(a) airline ticket prices

(b) winner of a bowling tournament

(c) restaurants having a food-tasting party

(d) interview with a football player

(e) activities at a local craft fair

(f) review of an orchestra performance

(g) team soccer scores

(h) an article about Disneyland

(i) a time schedule of when the train leaves

(j) review of a local school play

Pretend you are the newspaper editor. Your job is to decide in which section of the newspaper to put each of the above items. Put the letter of the item under the name of the correct newspaper section in the box. Think about the purpose of the writing. Where in the newspaper would a reader look for this news? The first one has been done for you.

Entertainment	Sports	Travel
		(a) airline ticket prices

Concentrating on the Purpose
of Writing

Before you write, you should ask yourself these questions:

- "What is the purpose of my message or main idea?"

- "Who will read my message?"

Think about the answers to these questions before you start writing.

Below, you must make some writing choices. Put an "X" in front of the writing plan that you think works best to communicate the main idea.

Main Idea #1: *How you made a kite in art class*

Readers: *Other schoolchildren*

- _____ Plan 1:   Describe what the weather was like on the day
  that you made the kite, what you were wearing,
  and where the school art room is located.

- _____ Plan 2:   Clearly explain the materials needed, and
  describe each how-to step from the beginning
  to the end of making the project.

Main Idea #2: *An imaginary story about an adventure you had with your kite*

Readers: *All students who read the school newspaper*

- _____ Plan 1:   Give details about the first time you flew a real
  kite, describe people who helped you fly it, and
  tell how much fun you had doing it.

- _____ Plan 2:   Pretend you flew your kite from the top of the
  Empire State Building. Describe how you think
  things would look from this height. Include
  details about how the kite flew and how you
  managed to get it down.

For Main Idea #3, you must make your own writing plan. Think about the purpose of the writing. Think about the person who will read your writing.

Main Idea #3: *You want permission to fly your kite at school*

Reader: *Your teacher*

• Writing Plan

_____

_____

_____

_____

_____

Now think of another main idea that you could write about. List the main idea and the reader of the idea below. Then describe your writing plan. (See page 36 for examples.)

Main Idea: _____

Reader: _____

• Writing Plan

_____

_____

_____

_____

Writing Assignments With a Focus on Content

If you were a reporter for a newspaper, your editor would advise you to do the following:

- "Think of your reading audience."

- "Keep your writing interesting by providing details that readers want to know."

Pretend that you are a reporter for a newspaper. Choose one of the following assignments and write about it. Don't forget that each assignment has a specific purpose and that readers will be reading each article for different information.

1. Write about the history of your school. Your report should include information such as when the school was built and how it got its name. Provide details about school traditions and activities. (New students will read this report.)

2. Report on a school sports event. Present some of the information from the point of view of one of the participants in the event. (Students at your school will read this.)

3. Write a review and recommendation for a children's movie. (You should let parents know if you suggest seeing the movie or not.)

4. Write an editorial to convince your principal that students should attend school only 3 days a week. (Include clear facts to persuade the principal that this is a good idea.)

5. Describe a good place to have fun in your community. (Write for readers who are new to your town.) Write about the special things that happen in this place and include the things a visitor would expect to see, smell, touch, and hear when visiting.

6. Write about something funny that happened to you or someone you know. Describe what happened so that any reader can experience the event and have a good laugh.

3

Word Choice

$\mathcal{W}$hy do I choose the words that I do when I write?

I must choose words carefully so that readers understand exactly what I mean.

I choose words that make my meaning clear, and I leave out unnecessary words.

I make my writing interesting when I

- Choose words that put my personality into my writing
- Select words that paint a sharp picture in the reader's mind
- Use action verbs and nouns that are precise
- Describe details with specific adjectives
- Write with a variety of words
- Take everyday words and use them in new ways
- Create new words and use them in imaginative ways
- Learn new ways to put words together

Looking at Pictures and Using Descriptive Adjectives

Look at the pictures below. Choose two pictures. Write three descriptions by each picture you choose. Use words that are creative and that describe the details. One example is done.

Presidential portrait
Bearded gentleman
Serious facial expression

Combining Pictures to Create New Words

Look at the pairs of pictures below. Write a word that fits under each picture. Then read the two words out loud together to find the new word that you have just created. Think of a fun way to use this new word in a sentence. Write the sentence.

Examining Creative Word Choices in Literature

Sometimes, authors make imaginary descriptions by putting real words together. Other times, authors make up imaginary words to describe or name things that aren't real.

Below is a list of imaginary words that authors Shel Silverstein and Roald Dahl made up. If you have read the books *A Light in the Attic, Where the Sidewalk Ends,* or *The BFG,* you may have seen these words before.

Make up a definition after each word by writing what you think the word means. You may want to look in the books to see what the authors meant when they used each word.

Frigiditydaire

Peppermint wind

Squishy touch

Hurk

Marshmallow earmuffs

Frobscottle

Snozzcumbers

Make up three imaginative words of your own below. Next to each word, tell what it means.

1. _____

2. _____

3. _____

Selecting Descriptive Words

Look at each pair of the following words. Circle the word that paints a sharper picture.

1. playground   park
2. Mercedes Benz   car
3. candy   M&M's®
4. writer   reporter
5. said   explained
6. deadline   time
7. game   Nintendo®
8. cousins   people
9. summer   season
10. Coca-Cola®   cold drink
11. snack   nachos
12. ate   swallowed
13. news broadcast   show
14. story   editorial
15. sport   baseball

16. hot day   sizzling day
17. hit   punched
18. ran   jogged
19. look   examine
20. shoes   sandals
21. writing   journalism
22. dessert   blueberry pie
23. Classified ad   picture
24. flower   carnation
25. tired   exhausted
26. moving child   squirming toddler
27. cucumber   vegetable
28. title   headline
29. champion   winner
30. moved   slithered

Making Verb Choices to Put Readers in the Center of Action

To hold the attention of your readers when you write, do the following:

- Use strong, specific verbs that put readers in the center of the action.

- Avoid using tired, common verbs that readers hear and see every day. Instead, use verbs that demonstrate exactly what you mean.

Read the following sentences and notice the underlined verbs. Put an "X" by the sentences that have strong verbs to help you see the action more clearly.

_____ When she <u>discovered</u> that there was no charcoal to <u>grill</u> the steaks, she <u>dashed</u> to the store.

_____ When she <u>saw</u> that there was no charcoal to <u>cook</u> the steaks, she <u>went</u> to the store.

_____ The old woman <u>walked</u> up the hill and then <u>fell</u> on the ice.

_____ The old woman <u>crept</u> up the hill and then <u>tumbled</u> on the ice.

_____ Because the room <u>had</u> junk in it, he <u>had</u> to <u>go</u> around the boxes.

_____ Because the room <u>overflowed</u> with junk, he <u>scrambled</u> around the boxes.

Write three sentences below with specific action verbs.

_____

_____

_____

_____

Recopy each of the following sentences. Replace the overused, underlined verbs with verbs from the "Verb Bank" to show the action more clearly.

1. The dog <u>moved</u> through the water, <u>went up</u> the stairs, and <u>ate</u> his food.

2. He <u>hit</u> the ball and <u>looked</u> at it as it <u>went</u> over the fence.

3. She <u>held</u> the baby as the packages <u>fell</u> to floor. The noise <u>woke</u> the baby, and he <u>cried.</u>

1.

2.

3.

Verb Bank

crashed	gazed	mounted	cradled
sloshed	startled	shrieked	gulped
soared	walloped	waded	smacked

Now start a "New Verb Bank" of your own by writing a new action verb on the lines provided in the box below.

New Verb Bank

moved:	went up:	ate:	hit:	looked:

went:	held:	fell:	woke:	cried:

Choosing Picturesque Adjectives, Nouns, and Verbs

When you write, readers will be able to hear, smell, taste, and feel what you describe

- If you use clear and precise descriptive words that help put readers in the experience

- If you avoid boring words that give only unclear, general information

Mark the more descriptive story below by circling the verbs, nouns, and adjectives that help you picture the story. Then write about something that happened to you.

1. One time, I had to go to the doctor to get a shot. It was after I cut my finger. We drove there in the car. We went into the big building. It scared me. My mom answered lots of questions. Then a nurse in a uniform took me into a room. Then she got a big needle. I didn't like the needle. Then she gave me a shot, and they fixed my finger. It wasn't bad. Then we went home.

2. When I was six years old, I had to rush to my doctor's office to get a shot. I sliced open my thumb on the jagged edge of an old tin can. We raced down our street with the tires on our car squealing like a pig. When we hurried into the huge clinic, I thought to myself, "I'd rather be any place but here!" My mother had to answer so many questions that I thought, "I'm going to bleed to death before they sew my finger back on!"

   Fortunately, a nurse soon came and escorted us to the treatment room. She was dressed from head to toe in white, and she was gentle as an angel. I changed my mind when she got out a needle like an elephant syringe. She helped me relax by breathing in and out, so the shot was just like a pinch. After that, the doctor wrapped my thumb with a special bandage that looked like a butterfly. When we were finished, we drove home at a more leisurely pace.

Writing With Similes to Create Sharp Images

When you write, you may help readers form pictures in their minds by comparing things. When you use the words *like* or *as* to show how two things are similar, you are using a word choice that is called a *simile.* Read the underlined similes below.

> When I was six years old, I had to rush to my doctor's office to get a shot. I sliced open my thumb on the jagged edge of an old tin can. We raced down our street with <u>the tires on our car squealing like a pig.</u> When we hurried into the huge clinic, I thought to myself, "I'd rather be anyplace but here!" My mother had to answer so many questions that I thought, "I'm going to bleed to death before they sew my finger back on!"
>
> Fortunately, a nurse soon came and escorted us to the treatment room. She was dressed from head to toe in white, and <u>she was gentle as an angel.</u> I changed my mind when she got out <u>a needle like an elephant syringe.</u> She helped me relax by breathing in and out, so <u>the shot was just like a pinch.</u> After that, the doctor wrapped my thumb with a special bandage that looked like a butterfly. When we were finished, we drove home at a more leisurely pace.

Can you hear the noise that the car tires make? Finish this simile:

The wind howled like _____.

What does the writer feel when she says the nurse was "gentle as an angel"?

Those emotions change when the writer describes "a needle like an elephant syringe." What do you think the writer felt like then?

Finish this simile:

She was frightened as _____.

Understanding How Word Choice Changes Meaning

When you write,

- Choose words that wake up readers and capture their imaginations
- Make careful word choices
- Remember that variety is important, but think about the exact meaning of a word
- "Say what you mean and mean what you say!"

Your word choice can shape or change the meaning of your story.

Read the groups of sentences below and follow the directions after each set.

1. Matthew agreed that the newspaper story would be finished by today.
2. Matthew demanded that the newspaper story be finished by today.

Circle the verb that means "Matthew knew when the story had to be finished." Underline the verb that means "The story must be finished today."

3. Sarah looked at the menu and then mumbled her order to the waitress.
4. Kaitlin squinted at the menu and then stated her order to the waitress.

Which girl may have trouble with her vision? What word gave you this clue? Which girl will the waitress have a harder time hearing? What word gave you this clue?

5. The boat disappeared beneath the murky water.

6. The bottle fell into the clear water.

Would you have a harder time finding the bottle or the boat? Write down the verb and the descriptive adjectives that helped you decide which object would be harder to find.

Writing Creatively With Onomatopoeias

An *onomatopoeia* is a word that imitates the sounds connected with an object or imitates the actions connected with an object. Here are some examples:

The engine *sputtered* to a stop.

The logs *crackled* in the fireplace.

The paint ran out of the overturned can and hit the ground with a *splat.*

You can have fun writing with onomatopoeias. You can even make up your own to describe the way things sound or appear when they are in action. One writer was asked to describe pictures flashed on a screen by a movie projector. But the projector made so much noise that she wrote, "I was busy listening to the rerrrrrr-ing sound in the background, and I didn't notice the pictures." "Rerrrrrr-ing" was the onomatopoeia the writer used to describe the sound of the movie projector.

Here is a list of some other onomatopoeias: *murmur, crunch, squish, buzz, crash, kerack, ping, boom, bop, shatter, clunk, chomp, rumble, roar, snort, splash, snatch, slam, slurp, whizz, yank, umph, squawk, sssshhhhh, pop, rasp, creak, whirr, mmm, and waahh.*

Name or make up two other onomatopoeias. Then write four sentences below using your own onomatopoeias or choosing ones from the list above.

_____

_____

_____

_____

Playing With Puns

One of the most important writing tools that you have is your ability to choose words and place them in any order. You can create new meanings and new ideas for readers.

A fun way to create new meanings is to write a pun.

- A pun is a play on words.

- You use a word that could mean two different things to a reader. Or you use words in a way that makes a joke for the reader.

Here are two examples:

I get a <u>kick</u> out of <u>soccer.</u>

<u>Astronauts</u> are <u>out of sight.</u>

One writer wrote, "My favorite thing that my mother cooks is German pancakes. But she never cooks German shepherds." The writer was able to make this pun because there are both pancakes called "German" and a type of dog that has "German" in its name.

Another writer wrote, "The idea of special rules for the sewer treatment plant created a stink." The pun here is that "to create a stink" can mean two things. So, when the author wrote, "created a stink," she was joking that the sewer plant smelled bad and also that people were upset about special rules.

In the following sentences, underline the words that are necessary to make the pun.

I'm hooked on fishing.   Safety is no accident.

Baseball is a big hit.   Swimmers are all wet.

Now write a pun of your own.

Considering Regional Differences in Word Choice

You must think about the audience that you are writing for when you make word choices. People from different regions of the world, or even the same country, may use different words to mean the same thing. These regional differences in the use of language are called *dialects*. Below are examples of words that people from different places might use to name the same object.

United States	*Great Britain*
French fries	chips
operating room	theatre
merry-go-round	helter-skelter
gasoline	petrol

Western United States	*Eastern United States*
submarine sandwich	hero or hoagie
porch	stoop
beach	(sea)shore
pop	soda

Think of four words that are familiar to people in your area but that might not be known by people from other regions of the United States. Write them below with a brief definition.

_____

_____

_____

_____

Deciding When a Word Choice Is Appropriate

One word choice that you can make is called *slang*. Slang

- Is language that is used in casual and playful speech

- Can be associated with a particular group of people

- May change the original use of a word

- Tends to change over time—words that are popular are replaced with other words

You must consider when it is appropriate to use slang. You might use slang when you write fiction because that is the way your fictional characters speak. You might also use slang when you write a letter to a personal friend. You would not be correct to use slang in a formal report or a business letter.

Below are some slang terms that are used in the newspaper business:

Off the record: when a reporter asks a question but agrees not to use the information discussed unless he finds the information somewhere else (A reporter never uses a quote from an answer that is given off the record.)

Graf: a paragraph

Dead: writing copy that has been set and proofread

Folo: (pronounced follow) a secondary article on the same subject as the main article

Hyping a story: writing a story with such pizzazz that the truth may be exaggerated

Tabloid: a term now used to refer to a newspaper that prints sensational stories (Originally, *tabloid* meant a newspaper that was the size of a magazine.)

On another paper, write five of your favorite slang words or expressions and definitions.

4

Sentence Fluency

Why do I put words together in the order that I do?

Even though I want my writing to stand out, I want it to stand out in a good way.

I want to put words together in ways that make sense to readers.

I want to clearly communicate my ideas.

I want to create on paper language that is smooth sounding and natural.

I write sentences that are smooth and easy to read when I

- Practice using different kinds of sentences
- Start sentences in different ways
- Combine words in sentences that vary in length and rhythm
- Write sentences that flow easily off the reader's tongue
- Communicate the precise meaning that I want to write
- Proofread my work out loud to make sure that I have not left out words or combined them in a way that is awkward or difficult to understand

Examining Patterns

A pattern is a design or plan. When writers use words, they learn to write with rules. If you use words in patterns that sound pleasing to the ear, you are using a rule called sentence fluency. A fluent sentence

- Flows smoothly when it is read out loud

- Is the opposite of a tongue twister, which feels as if you are tripping over your tongue

Look at the patterns below. Read the sentences out loud. Now draw or write a two-line pattern that sounds pleasing to your ear.

I see **chickens and bees.**

I see **rabbits and trees.**

Writing Poetry

The following pictures make a poem. Read the poem out loud. It flows smoothly. On another paper, write or draw your own poem. Read it out loud for fluency.

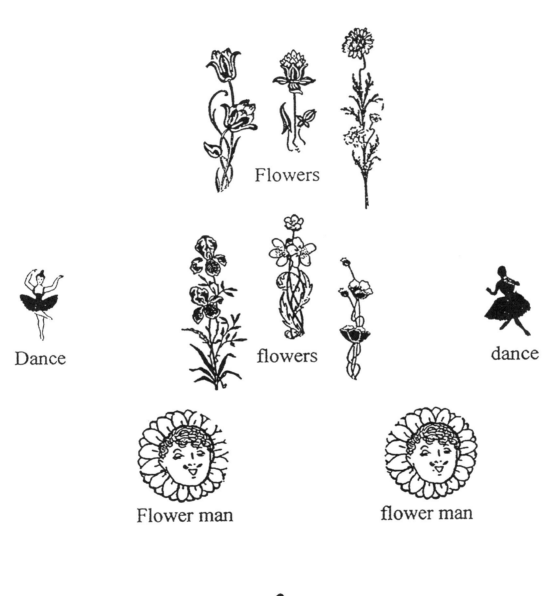

Flowers

Dance   flowers   dance

Flower man   flower man

U

dance

2

Reading and Writing Poetry to Hear Rhythm

Not all poetry rhymes. But in rhyming poetry, you hear smooth-flowing patterns. Read the following poem out loud. Circle words in your favorite line. Write your own poem.

Flower Child

When I was just a child,
I used to stare and gaze,
Upon the many flowers,
Upon the many days.

I used to walk through gardens,
Of a child's dreams,
Where pansies bordered rivers,
And daisies lined the streams.

There were vivid colored petals,
One of every hue,
From pinks and reds and purples,
To bright and brilliant blues.

Sometimes I'd sit to ponder thoughts,
As the time flew by.
I'd stop and smell the roses,
'Till stars twinkled in the sky.

And when the time had come for me,
I'd lie down in my bed,
And dream of things that I had done,
And things that lie ahead.

Reading and Writing Poetry to Hear Fluency

When you read them out loud, many poems allow you to hear the smooth way that words flow together in sentences. Read the following poem and watch for writing terms in it.

A Writer Wannabe

"So when you grow up, what do you want to be?"

Teacher asked Joshua Mordick McKenzie.

"That's easy," he said. "To write a book or story,

One that wins a prize and brings plenty of glory."

Disaster struck before he wrote a single word,

His writing *voice* ran away where it couldn't be heard,

His *ideas* got lost at a writer's *convention,*

And, oh, the *word choice* Josh muttered—I can't mention!

Josh knew that writers need more than paper and pen

And *organized* copies in the writing bin.

Poor Josh found out some author's plans aren't meant to be.

Instead of writing fame, he caught in-*fluency*!

––––––––––

SOURCE: Kathy Kirk, 1999. Not previously published.

Fluency means the effortless flow of language, whereas influenza is an illness. The writer makes a joke about Joshua by saying, "he caught influency." Most readers can still understand the poem, despite the nonsense word "in-fluency."

You may want to read some other fun poems, such as those by poet Shel Silverstein. Then on another paper, write your own poem to tell a story. Use real or made-up words that flow smoothly.

Exploring Fluent Sentence Structure

- A sentence is a group of words that expresses a complete thought.

- A sentence always has a subject, a noun that the sentence is about, and a verb, which shows either an action or a state of being.

- You must include these parts of speech to communicate clearly and smoothly in fluent sentences.

Read the following sentences. The subjects and verbs are underlined. Put an "X" over the subject and circle the verb.

1. I write a newspaper column.
2. The *Keizertimes* is my newspaper.
3. The book was exciting.
4. Editors like well-written articles.
5. In the comics, Garfield eats lasagna.
6. John wrote a story about baseball.

The following sentences have made-up words in them. You should still be able to tell which word is the subject and which word is the verb. Read the sentences and put an "X" over the subject and circle the verb.

1. The weatherman predicted a floopy storm.
2. Reporters scruttletot around town.
3. Did you osken a newspaper?
4. Dromebeekos give free candy.
5. The elephant is a hooglygot.
6. Ootwhoos eat six meals every day.

On another sheet of paper, write six sentences of your own. Write sentences that flow smoothly when you read them out loud. They should include both a noun and a verb and should express a complete thought. Have fun and use made-up words if you like.

Distinguishing Between Fragments and Complete Sentences

- A sentence is a group of words that expresses a complete thought.

- A fragment is an incomplete group of sentence parts.

To make your writing flow smoothly and clearly, you should write complete sentences. You should not write sentence fragments.

Choose the complete sentences below by marking "S" next to them. Mark the fragments with the letter "F."

_____ He was sleeping in the shade.

_____ Threatened to flood everything in sight.

_____ The creek that runs by my house made a refreshing splashing sound.

_____ To welcome us home.

_____ After rolling in the sack of flour.

_____ Made a refreshing splashing sound as it rounded the corner of the house.

_____ The dog looked like a black shadow after falling into the bucket of tar.

_____ Barked with joy.

_____ He jumped in the ice-cold water.

_____ The cat meowed.

_____ Pretended to ignore us.

You will notice that both sentences and fragments can vary in length. Each can be either long or short. A sentence will always have a subject and a verb and will present a complete thought or idea. This gives the sentence fluency.

Joining Fragments to Create Fluent Sentences

When you write, try to use different "sizes" of sentences.

- You can write short sentences called simple sentences.

- You can write a sentence that combines several simple thoughts by joining them together, and this is called a compound sentence.

The following are a number of sentence fragments (incomplete sentences) or sentence parts. On another paper, combine them to form simple and compound sentences. Write at least five sentences of each. There are several examples in the box after the sentence parts.

the creek bed   cat   under the hot summer sky   in the shade

looked like a dusty ghost   pretended to ignore us   by my house

dog   but   after rolling in the sack of flour   overflowed its banks

meowed   he   on this dark and stormy night   to welcome us home

and threatened to flood everything in sight   the

looked like a black shadow after falling into the bucket of tar

the creek   lonesome   very sad

made a refreshing splashing sound   and   feeling neglected   looked

barked with joy   he was   that meanders   ate quickly   still looked

jumped into the water   his eyes   our   slept lazily   my

My cat meowed to welcome us home.

The creek bed looked like a dusty ghost under the hot summer sky.

Our dog barked with joy, but his eyes still looked very sad.

He was feeling neglected, and he pretended to ignore us.

Selecting Fluent Sentences

When you write fluent sentences, you create sentences that are "easy on the reader's ear." This means that the sentences have words that sound natural and go together well. One of the best ways to proofread your work is to read it out loud.

Read the following pairs of sentences out loud. Choose the sentence that sounds more pleasing to your ear and place an "X" next to it. Think about what makes one sentence fluent and what makes the other sound choppy, unclear, unnatural, or just boring.

_____ 1.   Stephanie Rogerson is a delightful and typical four-year-old.

_____ 2.   Stephanie Rogerson is a girl and so she is nice and so she is a four-year-old.

_____ 3.   People in baseball think it's sort of likely that the team can do good next year.

_____ 4.   As they say in the baseball trade, "Just wait until next year!"

_____ 5.   Jake's interest in music began when he was in kindergarten.

_____ 6.   Jake he liked music. I mean it started. He started liking. It was in kindergarten.

_____ 7.   A "sudden death" play-off makes soccer a very interesting game.

_____ 8.   In soccer they can make a play called a "sudden death" and you like to watch it.

_____ 9.   There's lots of kinds of choices of toys that you can buy at that there store.

_____ 10.   The toy store sells a variety of unusual and creative toys.

Looking at Techniques for Fluent Writing

To make your writing interesting and fluent,

- Vary the rhythm of your writing by mixing short and long sentences together

- Use transition words to move smoothly from one paragraph or thought to the next

- Start sentences with different words

Read the following paragraphs for examples. Answer the questions on another paper.

> Casey Martin is a young man from Eugene, Oregon. He has a painful leg disorder. He was born with it. It keeps him from walking the entire length of a golf course. This is a problem because Casey wants to play professional golf and needs to use a golf cart.
>
> The Professional Golf Association didn't want to let Casey use a golf cart because the rules require that all golfers walk. A judge decided that Casey could use a golf cart in competition. This judge agreed that Casey just wants to play golf, not have special rules.
>
> Another young man who wants the chance to do things is a high school freshman named Jake Stai. Two of the nicest things about Jake are his caring attitude and his sense of humor. Jake has cerebral palsy. His brain works a little differently from yours or mine. When Jake wanted to be in the marching band at school, he worked extra hard to learn to march and play his horn because he has some trouble with coordination and speech.
>
> We should admire people such as Casey and Jake. They remind us that all people have strengths and weaknesses. With determination, we all have the ability to succeed.

Write down the longest and the shortest sentences. How many words are in each one?

Write each word that starts a sentence. How many sentences start with the word *the*? Write the transition words that move the reader from learning about Casey and introduce Jake.

Changing Sentences to Create Fluency

It is important to include both long and short sentences when you write.

- Long sentences give more information. Short sentences give your reader a chance to pause. The combination creates a rhythm to your written words. By using different lengths of sentences, you make your writing more fluent or "smooth flowing."

- When you start sentences with different words, you also create fluent writing.

Read the paragraph below. Write down the number of sentences that begin with the word *he*. Write down the number of words in the longest and shortest sentences.

1. Casey Martin is a young man. He is from Eugene, Oregon. He has a painful leg disorder. He was born with it. He can't walk an entire golf course. He has a problem. He wants to play golf. He needs to use a golf cart.

Now read the second paragraph. It is more fluent because it has both short and long sentences and different word choices at the beginning of most sentences.

2. Casey Martin is a young man from Eugene, Oregon. He has a painful leg disorder. Casey was born with a medical problem. It keeps him from walking the entire length of a golf course. This is a problem because Casey wants to play professional golf and needs to use a golf cart.

Now, complete the following exercise.

Rewrite paragraph #3 below so that it is more fluent. Write sentences that are both long and short. Use a different word at the beginning of each sentence.

3. Jake Stai is another young man who wants a chance to do things. Jake is a freshman in high school and has a caring attitude and a good sense of humor. Jake has cerebral palsy, which means that his brain works differently from yours or mine. Jake wants to be in the marching band at school, so he has to work extra hard. Jake has to work hard because he has some trouble with coordination and speech.

5

Organization

Where do I start and when do I end when I write?

I understand that to be a good writer I must do the following:

- Find ways to think of main ideas
- Focus my main idea on a clear topic
- Develop a writing plan
- Write with a beginning, a middle, and an end
- Capture the reader's attention with an interesting beginning
- Include details that belong with my writing topic
- Share clear details that make sense
- Organize details in the order that events happened
- Write a conclusion that leaves the reader feeling satisfied

I understand that usually when I write, I am beginning with a rough draft or "sloppy copy." I know that I can make improvements each time I return to my writing and make a new draft.

Brainstorming to Develop Ideas and Topics

Choosing a topic or main idea can be hard work. Here is a suggestion: Keep a small notebook in which to collect writing topics. As ideas occur, you can write them down and save them to use later. Below is an example for recording ideas in list form to help you start writing. Look at #1 and then complete the empty lines in #2 and #3.

#1. Topics I could write about dogs:

1. The kinds of dogs that make the best pets
2. Proper care and feeding of puppies or adult dogs
3. Activities and games to play with dogs
4. The things you need to spend money on when you own a dog
5. Most popular names for dogs and why people choose them

#2. Topics I could write about sports:

1. _____

2. _____

3. _____

#3. Topics I could write about my family:

1. _____

2. _____

3. _____

Using Idea Webs to Focus a Topic

You may think of an idea that has too much information. To help narrow the idea,

- Brainstorm details and smaller focused topics that fit the idea

- Draw an idea web with your main idea in the center and details in the "spokes"

Look at the following examples. Then draw a web of your own. In the middle, write, "Things to collect for a hobby." Now add details and information to complete the web.

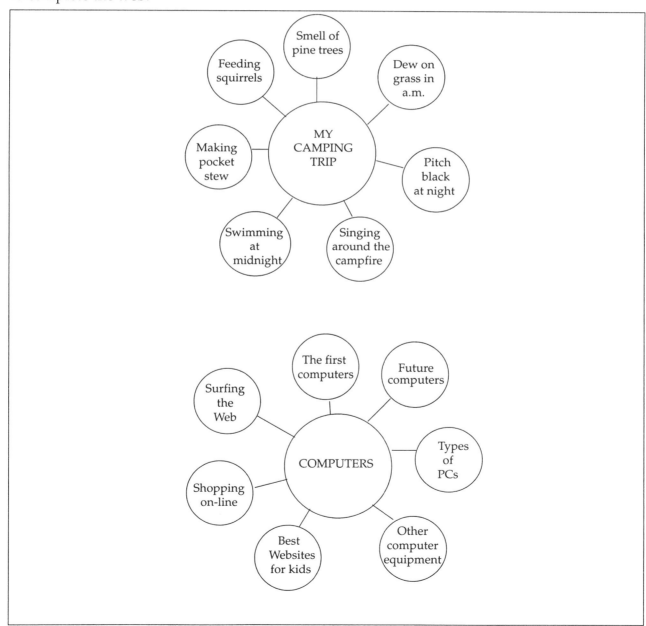

Selecting Focused Topics

Pretend that you are a reporter for a newspaper. Your editor has given you the following writing choices. Look at each group and put an "X" next to the topics that are focused on small, clear ideas. Put an "O" next to the topics that are about a very large subject.

_____ 1. Write an article about farming in America.

_____ 2. Interview a local boy about the work he does on his family's blueberry farm.

_____ 3. Do a report that lists the five concerns parents have about teenage drivers.

_____ 4. Write an article about the automobile industry.

_____ 5. Write a story about the toy most requested by third-grade boys.

_____ 6. Describe all the toys available at a large toy store.

_____ 7. Write about the American Football League.

_____ 8. Interview a local football star and ask how he broke his leg in a recent game.

_____ 9. Write about the oldest member in your family.

_____ 10. Write about all the original families who were the first to live in your state.

Developing a Writing Plan

Once you've brainstormed or talked with another writer to find a great writing topic, you will want to make a writing plan. You may use a list or an idea web to write down a sample of the important details. (See pages 67 and 68.)

After you decide which important details to include, you need to do three things:

- Think of a way to grab your reader's attention with your first sentence

- Think of experiences that you can use to illustrate the main points of your topic

- Think about a powerful way to end or conclude your writing

Look below to see how an author used these three steps in a writing plan.

A reporter and her family followed Mark McGwire's 1998 baseball season. She was impressed with McGwire's ability to break Roger Maris's home run record. She thought about how many people don't get any publicity, but they have to deal with difficulties that make them more of a "hero" than an athlete is. She also thought of her friend Glenn. She wrote an article about how Mark McGwire did an important thing when he broke the home run record. But the main idea of her story concluded, "Some heroes do more than hit the ball."

---

1. She decided to capture her readers' attention by commenting on Mark McGwire. At the same time, she introduced them to her friend Glenn. She wrote,

   Gary Gaetti, the Cubs' third baseman, got a bone-crunching hug after Mark McGwire's record-breaking 62nd home run. He said of McGwire, "The guy doesn't know his own strength." Like McGwire, my friend Glenn is a strong man—and fortunately for him, he *does* know his own strength.

2. Next, the reporter showed details that made her think that Glenn was a hero:

In 1997, Glenn was diagnosed with cancer. As Glenn fights his disease, he continues to live life as he always has—a hard-working, generous, and outgoing man. He often visits and encourages other patients. He trades recipes and his gourmet cooking secrets. He organizes his time to spend it with the people who mean the most to him.

Glenn deals with his cancer just as he faced the four open-heart surgeries that his youngest son has undergone. Glenn draws his strength from his earthly family and from the renewal he says he finds in his Father above.

3. The reporter finished with this conclusion:

In the plain light of everyday life, it seems pretty obvious that what Mark McGwire hit was, indeed, simply a baseball. If I'm going to grant "hero" status to anyone, I'll probably save it for my friend Glenn and his wife, Karla. They already know the score. They could pass a few tips to Mark McGwire and the rest of us about loving and valuing the people in our lives.

Think of a topic that you want to write about. On another paper, summarize your idea (the main details) in a paragraph and complete these three steps:

1. Write your opening sentence or sentences. Introduce your readers to your topic and capture their imagination. Make readers think, "I wonder what happens next!"

2. List experiences that are related to your topic. Include details that fit.

3. Write a conclusion that will satisfy your readers and that sums up your main idea.

Practicing Organized Writing

Below are several writing plans for organizing and writing about main ideas. Choose one of the numbered main ideas and write about it on another piece of paper. You may organize the idea and details as suggested, or you may develop your own writing plan.

For whichever plan you choose, do the following:

- Introduce your main idea with a strong lead that states the purpose of your writing.

- Write about one part of your main idea in each paragraph. Introduce each paragraph with a topic sentence and then support it with related details.

- Keep your writing interesting and ordered in a clear sequence that is easy to follow.

- Write a conclusion that summarizes your main idea.

1. Write a recipe for your favorite real or imaginary food. Be sure that you tell readers (a) what ingredients they will need, (b) what steps to follow and in which order, and (c) any information they need to know, such as oven temperature.

2. Write a description of your bedroom. (a) Give the readers a "tour" of your room by starting at your bedroom door and walking them throughout the area. (b) Point out your favorite things in the room and why you like to spend time there. (c) Tell your readers the changes you would like to make and why you can or can't make those changes to the room.

3. Tell readers about your favorite computer or board game. (a) Explain how to play the game. (b) Start with the information that they will need to know to begin. (c) Explain the reasons that they must perform certain steps. (d) Tell them what can go wrong. (e) Conclude with what you like best about the game.

Looking at the Three Parts of a Story

Every story has a beginning, a middle, and an end. Look at the pictures of the ballet dancer below. In the first picture, she is getting ready to dance. In the middle picture, she has started to dance. In the last picture, she is standing on one foot with her arms stretched to the sky.

Look at the other groups of pictures on this page. Write "1" by the picture that you think comes at the beginning of the story, "2" by the picture that comes in the middle of the story, and "3" by the picture that comes at the end of the story.

Looking at Transitional Words

This section contains three lists of words. The first list includes words to use at the beginning of a story. The middle list contains words to continue the story. The last list has words to write the end of the story. Look at the boxed example. Next look at the underlined words. On the lines underneath, write words that fit a story beginning, middle, or end.

One day	Next	Never again
I decided to straighten my doll collection. First, I washed the dolls.	I washed their clothes, dusted the shelves, and re-arranged things.	will I do everything all at once. It's too much work!

Beginning Words: **Middle Words:**   **End Words:**

<u>Once when</u>   <u>Soon</u>   <u>Finally</u>

_____   _____   _____

_____   _____   _____

_____   _____   _____

<u>The best thing</u>   <u>And then</u>   <u>Eventually</u>

_____   _____   _____

_____   _____   _____

_____   _____   _____

<u>Let me tell you</u>   <u>After that</u>   <u>In the long run</u>

_____   _____   _____

_____   _____   _____

_____   _____   _____

Using Transitional Words

You should write sentences in an order that makes sense. Use transitional words

- To take readers logically from one thought to the next
- To give readers a clue to the sequence of events and the changes that occur in a piece of writing

For example,

Beginning words: *one time, once upon a time, at first,* and *when it started*

Middle words: *next, after, soon, then,* and *in addition*

End words: *eventually, in the end, finally,* and *in conclusion*

Put "1," "2," or "3" by each of the sentences that follow so that you have numbered them in the correct sequence (or order).

_____ After I discovered that I couldn't get into my car, I went back to the store.

_____ One time, I pushed a cart full of groceries to my car only to discover I'd locked my keys inside.

_____ Finally, I explained what I had done and asked if I could keep my groceries in the store refrigerator.

_____ Whenever I slipped and called one of the girls by her real name, Stephanie would correct me.

_____ Shortly after her arrival, Stephanie announced, "I'll be the mother, I'm Meg. Sarah, you'll be the daughter, and your name is Emily."

_____ Once my daughters baby-sat our neighbor Stephanie at our house.

On another paper, write three sentences. Use words to show the transition of events.

Focusing on Beginnings

> Just let me say right off the bat, it was a bike accident.
>
> It was about as "accidental" as you can get, too.
>
> Like Mick wasn't riding crazy. Or dodging in and out of traffic.
> And both his hands were on the handlebars and all that.

This is the way that author Barbara Park begins her story in the book *Mick Harte Was Here.* Do these sentences make you want to read more about this story?

What two things do you know after reading just the beginning 46 words?

Name one of the characters in the book and tell what you think happened.

Think about some of your favorite books. Discuss what you remember about the beginning of one of those books. Write down an opening line that you remember.

If you want to be a good writer, you need to get your readers' attention right from the beginning of your work. You must also give readers a clue about your main idea.

Creating Sensational Beginnings

- Newspaper reporters use a writing technique called a *lead* to make the beginning of stories clear and interesting.

- Read the way the following pretend newspaper stories start. Look in parenthesis for the type of lead the reporter used to create interest.

"When the roof began to collapsed, I saw a river of what looked like lava running straight at me. I'll never make it out alive, I thought."

Fireman Robby Straw did make it out alive, after responding to a 6-alarm fire. (A direct quote, which creates a strong image, is followed by details of the event.)

Five hundred tubas take up an entire room of his house, but Ryan Long doesn't mind. The musician has been playing the tuba since age 8 and collecting them every since then. He will perform in concert on Saturday. (An interesting fact is followed with other details.)

Would you be willing to feed eight tiny reindeer year-round if they worked only one night a year? That's not a question that Susan Long struggles with. Her reindeer work every day of the year. (Reporter asks a question that fits with the main idea of his story.)

Pretend that you are a writer for a newspaper. The headline of your story reads, "Nightmare comes true when tarantula escapes local pet store." On another sheet of paper, write the first paragraph of this story. You get to decide what happened, but your lead should (a) include details that match the headline and give readers a clue to what the story is about and (b) immediately capture your readers' attention.

Writing "Reader-Catching" Leads

In newspaper writing, a lead is the first few sentences or paragraphs that a reporter writes. The purpose of a lead is

- To introduce a story to readers in a way that will make them want to read more

- To alert readers to the main idea

Look at the following groups of paragraphs. Above each group, the main idea is listed in parenthesis. Circle the paragraph that best introduces you to the main idea and makes you want to read more of the story.

(The First Day of School)

1. You only think you've had bad days! Were you ever sitting in a room full of people that you just met and then discover that your shirt is on inside out, you have on one blue shoe and one black shoe, and you have a big hole in the toe of your kneesock? Well, that's exactly what happened to me. And that was one of the better things about my first day of middle school! When I tell you the rest of the story, you won't believe the things that happened to me on that first day of school.

2. Then summer was over. Then it was the first day of school. Then I had to go to my first day of school. Then my teacher started giving me work. And I thought about the time this summer. I had fun this summer. Especially when I went to the fair. I liked the fair, but the sun was really hot. It's hot in school, too.

(My Favorite Teacher)

3. I had a favorite teacher. My teacher was a man. My teacher was Mr. Hull. He was married to Mrs. Hull. She was a teacher, too, but she taught kindergarten and Mr. Hull taught high school English and he also helped coach. Some coaches are mean. I think Mr. Hull was nice. Some people are nice, but some are not so nice.

4. His friends called him "Toad" because he was short and squat, and, in some ways, he resembled a toad. We were allowed to use his nickname but only if we addressed him as Mr. Toad. I would probably have liked Mr. Toad no matter what—because even when I was 16, I loved to read and write. Mr. Toad became my favorite teacher. He was the high school English teacher who made me believe that I had a strong writing voice and something important to say.

Choose one of the topics above ("The first day of school" or "My favorite teacher"). Write a lead paragraph on another sheet of paper: (a) Give details that clearly communicate the main idea, and (b) draw your reader in with a creative writing lead.

Next write a second lead paragraph for a topic of your choice. Provide the information and details that (a) clearly introduce the topic and (b) make the reader want to read more about what you have written.

Underneath your second lead, write down the subject of your topic.

Summarizing With a Satisfying Conclusion

If you read your favorite book or story and found that someone had removed the last chapter, can you imagine how disappointed you would be? Suddenly, one of the most important parts of the story would be missing! To write well, you must finish with a conclusion. Ask yourself if you "wrapped up all the loose ends":

- Did I finish telling the story that I wanted to tell?

- Did I answer all the questions that my story created for the reader?

- Does my writing make sense the way that I have ended it?

- Did I forget to include something that would finish the story in a better way?

Read the following sentences. Author Barbara Park wrote them to conclude her book *Mick Harte Was Here.*

I stood up and looked at it.

I smiled.

Mick Harte was here.

And now he's gone.

But for twelve years and five months, my brother was one of the neatest kids you'd ever want to meet.

And I just wanted to tell you about him, that's all.

I just thought you ought to know.

What do you know about some of the main characters just by reading this conclusion?

According to her conclusion, why did the author write this book?

Writing Clear Conclusions

When you write a conclusion, you should summarize your main idea. To make sure that you have communicated what you intended to write, ask yourself the following:

- Did I finish telling the story that I wanted to tell?

- Did I answer all the questions that my story created for the reader?

- Does my writing make sense the way that I have ended it?

- Did I forget to include something that would finish the story in a better way?

Read the following conclusion to a newspaper story. Answer the questions that follow.

Despite being late for the most important game of his life, Blake Holder was sent onto the field just in time. With two minutes to spare, he kicked the game-winning 28-yard field goal. The high school crowd went crazy, and even Blake forgot about being mad.

"After all," he said laughing, "I was the only one who drove the car last night, so I guess I can't blame my mom that we ended up stranded on the roadside today. You can bet I'll check the gas gauge before next year's homecoming game!"

Circle the detail words that tell what kind of a game Blake played in and how it ended.

According to this conclusion, why did Blake almost miss playing in the game?

Would you say that the game had a happy ending? Why?

Pretend that you are just finishing a story about a tarantula that escaped from a pet store. On another paper, summarize the ending that concludes your story. Include specific details.

Wrapping Up Writing

You should conclude your writing with a paragraph or two that

- Reminds your readers of your main idea

- Summarizes your information in a satisfying way

Read the following paragraphs. The first two were written about the first day of school, and the second two were written about a favorite teacher. Circle the paragraphs that make the best conclusion for the topic. Put an "X" by the paragraphs that have too many details that don't fit together and that don't give the reader a clear conclusion of the main idea.

(The First Day of School)

1. _____ So, I said to Mary, "Well, that was the first day of school. It was the first day of middle school." She agreed that it was the first day for her and her brother and my sisters, too. My mother went shopping today with a friend and to have lunch. My mother always has lunch with her friend on the first day of school. It is the end of her summer also. She is not so sad because she does not have to go to school. Like I did today.

2. _____ Yes, my first day of middle school was pretty disastrous. I left school feeling awful about my appearance, sad that I had lost my wallet, and sure that no kids could have a worse day if they tried! But the really amazing thing was that I *knew* tomorrow would be better. I was going home and putting out fresh clothes right away so I wouldn't start my second day of school on the wrong shoe—or at least they would be shoes of the same color!

(A Favorite Teacher)

3. _____ The amazing thing about Mr. Toad was that he found something special in all his students. He helped us find the best part of ourselves. He taught us to give things back to our community. Mr. Toad always encouraged me to write. He helped me believe that my writing could change the world around me. Sometimes now, when I read something that I have written, I realize that, in a way, part of my writing still belongs to my favorite teacher, Mr. Toad. He nurtured my love of written language, but he also helped me find my voice and taught me to use it well.

4. _____ Yes, he was a nice teacher, and Mrs. Hull was nice, too. They lived in the green house, but it was not close to my house. Sometimes, teachers live close to you, but not this time. Mr. and Mrs. Hull did not live close to me. Sometimes, I wish they did because they are nice teachers. I lived by a teacher in a blue house once. But they have a yellow house and a nice dog, too. Mr. Hull was one of my favorite teachers.

On another paper, list a main idea and then write a conclusion for it. Be sure to

- Stick to your main idea
- Provide an ending that summarizes your topic

The Importance of Rewriting Drafts

Start your writing with a "sloppy copy" or "rough" first draft. With the rough draft,

- Include your main idea and the details that go with your main idea

- Then make necessary changes by rewriting (Making writing changes is called making a *revision.*)

Think of this word as "re-vision," which means, "to see something again." Each time you write, try to "see again" what you want to communicate to readers. Make needed changes with each draft that you write. Save all drafts until you are finished.

With each revision, check for the following:

- An interesting beginning that introduces your main idea

- Specific details that support your topic

- Descriptive, interesting, and purposeful word choices (Look for missing words.)

- A conclusion that summarizes your main idea

- Punctuation and conventions that make your meaning clear to readers

Look at the following writing. You will see changes the author made with the revision.

(Rough Draft)   The rest of salem enjoyed sunny days over the break. I played nurse and writer and so I didn't get much of a chance to go outside.

My dotter had her tonsils removed in decembr and had to stay in bed. She spend her time eating popsicles. I didn't have time to look outside. I was busy acting like the nurse that I used to be in the hospital. I went up and downstairs to take care of her.

Just when my daughter was feeling good, I had to stay in the bedroom. I wasn't sick but I writing. I I have a january time to send my writing workbook to my publisher and I still had lots of work to do. So I spent another week in the bedroom. Every day, I sat at the computer and wrote. I didn't go outside. I finished writing the workbok.

(Revision)   "Sunshine, what sunshine!" I wailed. It seems that while the rest of Salem was enjoying record sunny weather over the holiday break, I was too busy playing nurse and writer to get much opportunity to go outdoors.

My teenage daughter had her tonsils removed on December 18 and had to spend a week in bed recovering. She spent her time sucking on popsicles and ice cubes. With barely a glance out the window, I returned to my former life as a nurse, running up and down stairs to attend to Kaitlin.

Just when Kaitlin was feeling well enough to come out of the bedroom, I was stuck there myself. Fortunately, I wasn't sick, but I had writing to finish. Faster than you can say "Superman," I morphed from supernurse into Kathy Kirk, American writer. With a publishing deadline looming, I had to practically chain myself to my computer.

I didn't get to see much of the blue sky that week, but I did manage to complete the revisions on my workbook. When I send it to the publisher, I think I'll request a week on a tropical island. I need the sunshine that I didn't get to enjoy at Christmas time!

Write a rough draft about something you did during a winter break or vacation. Then write a second draft. Include all the steps listed earlier in this section as necessary in a revision.

Conventions

What symbols and rules do I use when I write?

I want to communicate with readers in a clear and interesting way, so when I write, I do the following:

- I use punctuation and writing conventions that help readers understand my meaning.

- I practice the proper use of commas, apostrophes, quotation marks, end-of-sentence punctuation marks, and capitalization of proper nouns.

- I choose verbs and nouns that go together correctly.

- I organize my writing so that I present information from a consistent point of view.

- I spell words correctly.

- I use references to help with my word choices. I practice so that I know how to use a dictionary and a thesaurus.

- I learn how to divide my topic into paragraphs and where to start and end each paragraph.

- I am adventuresome and don't worry about using perfect conventions in my first writing draft.

- I remember that I can edit my work at any time, but the most important time to focus on writing conventions is after I have focused on my main idea and details.

- I edit my own work and include the necessary changes in my writing revisions before I am satisfied that my writing is complete.

Understanding Writing Conventions

Read the following. Write an answer after each sentence. If you can't answer, then follow the directions in the box.

Xhpt qs ybuc npme*

Xhece db ybu gb tb schbbl*

Rewrite each of the sentences above. Use this code to replace letters and symbols:

X = W	C = R	Q = I
B = O	P = A	* = question mark (?)

Then answer the questions.

Writers must agree to use the same rules, also called *writing conventions*. If you don't use appropriate writing rules, you may not be able to communicate with readers. When you changed the sentences above, you used traditional ways to spell words. You also used a question mark to point out, "The writer is asking the reader a question." You can see why it is important to use writing conventions.

Investigating How Writing Conventions Affect Meaning

Writers use writing rules to make communication clear. Reporters use a special book that has an entire chapter on punctuation. The book tells reporters that they must use correct punctuation because incorrect punctuation can change the entire meaning of a sentence.

Read the following sentences, and then answer the questions.

A new restaurant serves cake watermelon ice cream and pie.

In an article, you write that the restaurant serves how many kinds of dessert?

A teacher's class includes Mary Ann Lisa Joe Bob and Michael.

During a fire, if the teacher can't find these pupils, how many students will you report as missing?

Is it cake, watermelon ice cream, and pie? or cake, watermelon, ice cream, and pie?

Is it Mary Ann, Lisa, Joe Bob, and Michael? or Mary, Ann, Lisa, Joe, Bob, and Michael?

Notice how the placement of the commas changes the meaning of each sentence.

A school reporter interviews a coach. The reporter had heard that the coach is quitting. When the reporter asks the coach if he is leaving the soccer team, the coach appears puzzled. Circle the correct sentence that the reporter should write to quote the coach. (The punctuation at the end of each sentence changes the entire meaning of the story.)

When asked if he is leaving the soccer team, the coach replied, "I am quitting soccer?"

When asked if he is leaving the soccer team, the coach replied, "I am quitting soccer!"

Identifying Common and Proper Nouns

Words used for everyday things are written with lowercase, or small letters, at the beginning. These words are common nouns. Examples include *book, dog, city,* and *spider.*

Words used to give the special names of people, places, or things are written with uppercase, or capital letters, at the beginning. These words are called proper nouns. In parenthesis are the common nouns, and underlined are examples of proper nouns:

(book)	Curious George
(dog)	Wishbone
(city)	New York
(spider)	Charlotte

Use common or proper nouns to write words by the following pictures. Then circle 10 common and 10 proper nouns in a newspaper.

Identifying Punctuation Marks at Ends of Sentences

When you write, you need to let readers know when to stop at the end of a thought. You do this by using punctuation marks at the ends of sentences. These marks also help readers understand the meaning of your sentence.

- Use a period to show where a statement ends. (.)
- Use a question mark to indicate that the reader must answer a question. (?)
- Use an exclamation point to show excitement or action. (!)

On the line at the end of each sentence, place correct punctuation marks to help readers understand the meaning of the thought.

I opened the door_____ A snarling giant jumped at me from the other side_____

Why was a giant hiding outside my front door_____

Would he try to eat me_____

I'll never know the answer to those questions_____

The ferocious-looking giant vanished into thin air right before my eyes_____

On another piece of paper, write three sentences that end with a period, three sentences that end with an exclamation point, and three sentences that end with a question mark.

Practicing the Placement of Commas

Commas are punctuation marks. They are clues that tell readers to pause when reading.

Here are three reasons to use commas when you write:

- To separate a series of items

- To separate compound sentences (A compound sentence combines two related thoughts that are joined together with the word *and* or *but*. Example: You will practice finding commas in sentences, and you will write sentences with commas.)

- To separate the numbers in a date

Place commas where they are needed in the following sentences:

I like to read about sports movies cooking and entertainment.

My dog barked with joy but he still looked very sad.

My editor wants me to write about skiing sledding skating and ice fishing.

He was feeling neglected and he pretended to ignore us.

Use commas to separate the numbers in a date, for example: Today is August 27, 2001. Use commas to separate the date from the rest of the writing in a sentence, for example: The date of the hurricane, February 4, 1998, was also her birthday. (You do not need to use a comma if you write only the month and the year, for example: She moved to Arizona in May 1968.)

On a paper, write two sentences with commas used properly to separate the numbers in a date. Then write two sentences with commas used properly to separate a series of items.

Showing Ownership and Creating Contractions

Apostrophes are punctuation marks. Use apostrophes when you write to

- Indicate when something belongs to someone
- Show that a letter has been left out when two words have been put together as a contraction (For example, *did not* becomes *didn't*, and *was not* becomes *wasn't*.)

Below are some rules to use when using an apostrophe to show possession.

You add an apostrophe and an *s* to the end of a singular noun and to a plural noun that does not end in *s*, for example,

<u>Kathy</u> wrote a book. <u>Kathy's</u> book is about children.

<u>Charles</u> is my favorite cousin. <u>Charles's</u> favorite cousin is Mark.

The <u>women</u> own a candy store. The <u>women's</u> candy is delicious.

You add only an apostrophe to the end of a plural noun that ends in an *s*, for example,

The <u>girls</u> like to play video games. The <u>girls'</u> best game is lost.

Don't use an apostrophe in the words *his, hers, mine, ours, theirs, whose,* or *yours.*

Rewrite the sentences below. Put apostrophes in the contractions and to show possession.

Lisas favorite food is popcorn. She loves to eat it but cant because she wears braces.

They invited Wess brothers to the movie. The boys evening was exciting.

The men took the boys to the football game. The mens game was over at nine.

Dont you remember if the book is Lauras or hers? Whose job is it to return the books?

On another paper, write five sentences that use apostrophes in the correct places.

Exploring the Use of Quotation Marks

Use quotation marks

- To make it clear that you are writing words that were actually spoken or written by someone else

- To surround the exact words of a speaker or writer, for example:

> I emphasized, "You must be on time for practice this afternoon."
> He replied, "I'm always on time for games."
> "Last week, you were late to three practices and the game," I reminded him.
> "That couldn't be helped!" he argued.
> "If you can't arrive on time," I threatened, "you may not get to play."
> "You are right," he agreed. "I should be on time like all the other players."

Write quotation marks where they belong in the following sentences. Look for words that show someone is speaking, and watch for punctuation that indicates that a quote is being used.

Matthew Turner won the fifth-grade spelling bee today. Matthew's teacher said, His hard work made all of the difference.

There are many good spellers in my class, so Matthew had strong competition. He practiced and practiced, and that helped him in the end, she explained.

Matthew replied, Many of the words were difficult, but I had studied hard all month.

Now that the spelling bee is over, Matthew said, I plan to spend more time outdoors.

On another paper, write four sentences that require quotation marks. Use the examples in the previous box to help you punctuate your sentences correctly.

Using Quotation Marks to Surround Special Words

You may use quotation marks to surround

- Some titles

- Nicknames

- Words used in a special sense

Here are some examples.

> Titles: When reporters write about books in the newspaper, they use quotation marks rather than underline a book's title.

E. B. White, author of "Charlotte's Web," will read at the bookstore.

> Nicknames

"Rose City" is the nickname given to the city of Portland, Oregon.

New Jersey is known as the "Garden State."

> Words used in a special sense

I watched Jake and his brother shoot hoops at the "basketball court." It's really only two worn-out nets tacked to different ends of the driveway, but the boys still have fun.

I "met" Erma Bombeck through a Sacramento newspaper that I was reading while visiting my grandmother. (The writer uses "met" to mean "became acquainted with Erma Bombeck's writing.")

On another paper, write three sentences that require quotation marks. Include quotation marks around words used as titles or nicknames and words used in a special sense.

Using Quotations to Add Interest to a Story

You can use quotations to add interest to your writing.

- Write quotation marks around the exact words spoken by the person.

- If you use a quotation, the quote should add a detail that makes sense and should move your story forward.

Read the following example.

A reporter wrote a story about children who played on a special baseball team. The team was formed for children who couldn't play on baseball teams with regular rules. The author wanted to show how much the team members cared for each other. The reporter could have written the following:

The children on the baseball team cared about each other very much.

Instead, she provided a detail that showed something that happened at a game. Then she used a quote to show readers how the teammates appreciate one another. She wrote,

Although Forrest arrived late to the last game, he will always remember the hero's welcome that he received. As he ran into the dugout, his teammates hugged him and shouted, "All right! Forrest is here!"

On a paper, write a paragraph or two about an event that happened. Include something that you clearly remember someone saying. Include a quote that (a) fits with your story and (b) moves the story along. Use quotation marks to show the words that were spoken.

Choosing Verbs and Subjects That Agree

To write sentences that flow smoothly and clearly communicate your meaning, you must choose verbs and subjects that belong together.

- Match a singular noun with a singular verb. For example, <u>He</u> <u>plays</u> ice hockey.

- Match a plural noun with a plural verb. For example, <u>They</u> <u>play</u> ice hockey.

Rewrite the sentences below. Cross out one of the underlined words and write a correct word above it so that the subjects and verbs belong together.

Did <u>you</u> <u>writes</u> this story? <u>Magazines</u> <u>prints</u> stories like this one.

<u>Newspapers</u> <u>has</u> a section about sports.

<u>Comics</u> <u>is</u> fun to read.

Baseball <u>players</u> <u>practices</u> hitting. The <u>coach</u> <u>don't</u> <u>eats</u> hotdogs.

Marathon <u>runners</u> <u>spends</u> many hours in training.

The <u>teacher</u> <u>think</u> the library has the book.

<u>Books</u> <u>costs</u> money.

On another paper, write three sentences of your own that show subjects and verbs that correctly go together.

Writing With a Consistent Point of View

A "point of view" is the way a story is presented to readers.

- Writing is in the "first person": The story is told as if you participated in the action with words such as "I am" or "we are."

- Writing is in the "second person": A story is told by talking directly to the reader and saying, "you are."

- Writing is in the "third person": The story is told as if talking about someone with words such as "he is," "she is," "it is," and "they are."

To communicate clearly with readers, you must write sentences from one point of view. Read the following examples.

First person: I was so excited about the fair. I spent days grooming my pig because I really wanted to win first place. When the blue ribbon was placed in my hand, I cried with joy.

Second person: You were so excited about the fair. You spent days grooming your pig because you really wanted to win first place. When the blue ribbon was placed in your hand, you cried with joy.

Third person: She was so excited about the fair. She spent days grooming her pig because she really wanted to win first place. When the blue ribbon was placed in her hand, she cried with joy.

The following paragraphs are confusing because the point of view changes in some sentences. Cross out **some** of the underlined words. Make the writing more clear by writing new words above the ones that you crossed out.

<u>I</u> like being the youngest member of <u>their</u> family. <u>My</u> grandparents take <u>him</u> camping and bring <u>me</u> special gifts. <u>We</u> read the comics together, and <u>it has</u> a good laugh. <u>I</u> love fishing with my grandpa, and <u>you</u> cook with my grandma. The only time that <u>we</u> don't like being the youngest is when <u>I</u> have to be the first one in bed!

"It's a girl!" the doctor shouted. <u>He</u> had just delivered my baby brother, and <u>it</u> made the announcement to all my family. <u>My family</u> was excited by the news, and <u>you</u> cried with joy. <u>I'm</u> going to love being a big sister, <u>we</u> thought.

Checking Spelling With Dictionaries

If you want readers to understand the meaning of your words, you must use and spell them correctly. First, use a dictionary to check spelling. Then ask another writer for help if you can't find the word.

Dictionaries have words listed from the beginning to the end of the alphabet (from *A* to *Z*). To use a dictionary, try these tips.

1. Try to sound out the beginning of the word and as many letters as you can.

2. Open the dictionary to the place that contains the first letter in your word.

3. Look at the word at the very top, left side of the page. This is the first word you will find in the left column (the first word on the page).

4. Look at the word at the very top, right side of the page. This is the last word you will find in the right column (the last word on the page).

5. Look at the first three or four letters in your word. See if they come in the alphabet between the first word and the last word on the page. If so, try to find your word on this page.

6. If the letters in your word do not come in the alphabet between the first word and the last word on the page, keep checking each page until you find your word.

For example, on a page with these words at the top

farm	father

The word *fast* would be on this page because it comes after *farm* and before *father.*

You would not find *fish*. *Fish* comes after *father,* so you must look after this page.

The word *fan* comes before *farm,* so you must look before this page.

Answer the following questions.

Do you think you would find *camel* on a page with these words at the top?

came	camera

If not, would you look before or after this page?

Do you think you would find the word *monkey* on a page with these words at the top?

mice	milk

If not, would you look before or after this page?

Use a dictionary to practice searching for these words: *ghost, volcano, nephew, ax.*

In the space below, copy the dictionary definition of one of the words above. Write down the page number on which this word is found in your dictionary.

Using Resources That Help With Writing

You can use other resources to help with spelling and word choice.

- A thesaurus is a book of synonyms. It lists words together that have the same or nearly the same meaning.

- Use a thesaurus to focus your writing with specific descriptive words.

Many computers have a built-in thesaurus and spell check.

Use a thesaurus to write additional descriptive words in the following lists:

| teacher | game | tell | dark |

| eat | toy | dance | magic |

You may use "spell check" if you write on a computer. Or you may want to start a dictionary/word list of your own. You can include words that you use frequently but need help with spelling or defining. Following is one example of a simple word list.

The 100 Most Common Words Used in English Writing

a	find	long	people	was
about	first	look	said	water
all	for	made	see	way
an	from	make	she	we
and	get	many	so	were
are	go	may	some	what
as	had	more	than	when
at	has	my	that	which
be	have	no	the	who
been	he	not	their	will
but	her	now	them	with
by	him	number	then	word
call	his	of	there	would
can	how	oil	these	write
come	I	on	they	you
could	if	one	this	your
day	in	or	time	
did	into	other	to	
do	is	out	two	
down	it	over	up	
each	like	part	use	

SOURCE: From Spandel, *Seeing With New Eyes* (1996, p. 185).

Editing Sentences in Paragraphs

When you write about a main idea, you must divide sentences into paragraphs.

- Each paragraph should contain only descriptions and details that fit with the topic of that paragraph.

Read the paragraphs below. Cross out the sentence that doesn't belong with the others.

You only think you've had bad days! Were you ever sitting in a room full of people that you just met and then discover that your shirt is on inside out, you have on one blue shoe and one black shoe, and you have a big hole in the toe of your kneesock? Well, that's exactly what happened to me. And that was one of the better things about my first day of middle school. I went to Kennedy Elementary School last year. When I tell you the rest of the story, you won't believe the things that happened to me on that first day of school.

No one likes going to the doctor's office to get a shot. But many people don't understand the importance of having their children immunized against childhood diseases. Some parents think that diseases such as measles, whooping cough, and polio no longer exist. Teenagers can break bones if they fall off a skateboard. These illnesses are still a very real threat to the health of children. When parents take their youngsters to get a shot or vaccination, they are helping to prevent the spread of life-threatening sickness.

Adding Punctuation to a Written Paragraph

Read the following paragraph. The punctuation has been removed. Fix the paragraph.

- Use some of the rules or conventions.
- Use capital letters and insert punctuation so that it makes sense to read.
- On another piece of paper, rewrite the sentences in paragraph form.

There are actually several ways to punctuate the paragraph and still be correct. Some of the choices depend on your own writing style.

you need to learn the rules of writing because you want to communicate with other people but you shouldnt be afraid of conventions if you think of writing simply as talking on paper you will worry less remember that you have interesting information to share so dont be afraid to write skilled writers know that they always have something new to learn

Separating Sentences Into Paragraphs

The topic of the following sentences is "The Writing Process." This title indicates that you will find information about a writing method. (The complete essay is on page 108.)

Place a paragraph symbol (¶) in front of four sentences to show where each paragraph should start. Look for transition words that indicate a change in thought. (See pages 73-74 in Chapter 5.) Separate the paragraphs by including only the details that belong together. Then rewrite the sentences on another paper, grouped together in four paragraphs.

1. In the first step of the writing process, the writer brainstorms to find a topic.

2. He may brainstorm by thinking, talking, reading, or observing.

3. After brainstorming and planning, the writer jots down information.

4. This rough draft is a "quick write," so he is not focused on doing perfect work.

5. This is simply the place where he begins writing.

6. Nothing is permanent at this point.

7. Next, he begins revising his rough draft.

8. He adds and subtracts sentences and focuses on details, word choice, sentence structure, and organization.

9. While he rewrites, he asks, "Does my paper have an interesting beginning, a logical middle, and a satisfying conclusion?"

10. Finally, he proofreads his work one last time.

11. He asks, "Have I clearly communicated my exact message?"

12. If no more changes are needed, he recopies the final draft.

Proofreading and Editing a Final Draft (Grades 3 and 4)

Use this guide when you are ready to proofread and edit a final draft. Read out loud to a friend. Ask yourself the following:

- Did I write so that my main idea is clear?
- Did I write things in order and so that they make sense?
- Did I use words such as *once, after that*, and *finally* to show a beginning, a middle, and an end?
- Did I include details that go with my main idea?
- Did I use correct punctuation at the beginning and end of sentences?
- Did I use commas correctly in dates and series of items?
- Did I underline words that I think might be spelled wrong?
- Did I make the needed changes?

After finishing the above and recopying your work neatly, you are ready to give your edited draft to your teacher.

Proofreading and Editing a Final Draft (Grades 5 and 6)

When you are ready to proofread and edit your final draft, you should read your entire paper out loud. Ask yourself the following:

- Did I write an opening paragraph that provides clues to my main idea and makes readers want to continue reading?

- Did I separate sentences into paragraphs by indenting? Do paragraphs fit together and provide specific details? Did I use transitional words?

- Did I write a closing paragraph that provides a conclusion for my main idea?

- Does my writing make sense, or do I need to add, change, or take out words to make the meaning clear?

- Did I use correct punctuation and capitalization?

- Did I circle words that may be misspelled? Did I underline words that should be replaced with more specific or more descriptive words?

- Did I make all the above changes that were needed?

Have a trusted writing partner or your teacher proofread your writing. Ask your proofreader if there are any suggestions for change. If not, then you are ready to rewrite your final draft.

The Writing Process

*In the first step of the writing process, the writer brainstorms to find a topic. He may brainstorm by thinking, talking, reading, or observing to develop an idea.

Next, he plans the way to present his idea. He thinks about the reading audience, the purpose of his writing, and the best way to write his message.

*After brainstorming and planning, the writer jots down information. This rough draft is a "quick write," so he is not focused on doing perfect work. This is simply the place where he begins writing. Nothing is permanent at this point.

When the writer completes this first draft, he spends time away from his work to clear his thinking. After taking this break, he returns and tries to see with new eyes what he has previously written.

*Next, he begins revising his rough draft. He adds and subtracts sentences and focuses on details, word choice, sentence structure, and organization. While he rewrites, he asks, "Does my paper have an interesting beginning, a logical middle, and a satisfying conclusion?"

He has been editing throughout the process, but the writer now focuses on proper spelling, punctuation, and writing conventions. He checks that paragraphs begin and end in logical places. He reads out loud and listens for smooth-flowing sentences and missing words.

*Finally, he proofreads his work one last time. He asks, "Have I clearly communicated my exact message?" If no more changes are needed, he recopies the final draft.

(The * indicates the paragraphs shown in the exercise on pages 104-105.)

Resource:
"Defining Values" Columns

The following excerpts appeared in my weekly "Defining Values" newspaper column published in the *Keizertimes* newspaper of Keizer, Oregon. Selections (and paraphrased selections) from these columns have been used as examples of the different writing traits throughout the workbook.

I have had positive feedback from classroom teachers who enjoyed reading the columns and enclose them for your reading pleasure. But I have also used the columns in their entirety to reinforce writing traits when working with academically gifted fifth and sixth graders.

I encourage educators and parents to use the columns with this population. It's fun for these students to read the titles of the columns and see my "slant" on a particular subject. Students in my writing workshops have eagerly tackled writing assignments on some of the column ideas such as persons with developmental disabilities, smoking, and cellular telephones.

The columns can be used to stimulate discussions about generating ideas, organizing material, and choosing words to sway readers and about how journalists incorporate their own styles and writing voices. I use actual newsprint copies of my column in workshops to point out some of the conventions of journalism. It also gives me an opportunity to remind young writers that although professional writers strive for perfection, sometimes errors created in editing or typesetting make it into print!

I strongly encourage users of this workbook to use their own community newspaper to engage students in exploring writing traits. The community newspaper is an inexpensive resource. Everything from classified ads to the sports section can be used to examine voice, ideas and content, word choice, sentence fluency, organization, and conventions.

Happy reading and writing!

AUTHOR'S NOTE: "Defining Values" columns by Kathy Kirk, 1998-1999, in the *Keizertimes*. Copyright © by Kathy Kirk. Used with permission. Columns started bi-weekly and soon became weekly.

Defining Values

Editor's note: This is the first column by Kathy Kirk, a longtime Keizer resident who will write bi-weekly about life in Keizer.

"Values" is one of those interesting words that, like beauty, often lie in the eye of the beholder. If you ask someone if a painting by van Gogh has value, he or she will quickly assure you that such a painting has economic worth that makes it a precious commodity.

Ask the mother of a college-aged student to trade that dusty box in the attic filled with 13 years' worth of scribbles, scrawls, and "artwork" for a van Gogh painting, and you might be surprised at her response.

Perhaps if you live in Los Angeles, New York City, or even a little closer to home—Portland—you won't have a clue to that mother's perspective. Years ago when I was commuting part-time to Portland and revealed that my hometown was Keizer, my coworker quipped, "Keizer, isn't that in the backwaters of Snailem?" She made it clear that Keizer didn't even merit the sophistication of an epithet aimed directly at it.

Ten and a half years later, my family is living in a Keizer that still doesn't boast a Nordstrom, a television station, or even a daily newspaper. We have lived here through the dubious time when Keizer could boast of being home to the largest middle school in the state; when the naming of the new baseball stadium, *Salem-Keizer Volcanoes*, rankled even those of its most ardent supporters; and when the issue of special zoning around the Willow Lake Treatment Plant first began to raise a stink. (Pun intended.)

When we outgrew our home on an acre on Verda Lane, our Realtor tried to entice us to South Salem and beyond. We were forced to examine the community we call home and make a judgment: Which was Keizer, a priceless treasure or a worthless box of junk? Three and a half years of living on a quarter acre near the new Clear Lake Elementary School have confirmed what we always knew about the identity of Keizer.

Bill Idelson, one of the writers of "The Andy Griffith Show," explained the show's success in an interview: "You know why everybody loves it? It's about man's humanity to man rather than man's inhumanity to man.... Here's a guy who treats his neighbors and the people on the street as if they were human beings."

Idelson would have found a wealth of material to write about in Keizer. What he didn't learn in "Mayberry" he could learn in the "backwaters of Snailem."

The value of a community rests in the way the community values its inhabitants—treats each individual with care, respect, and worth. The heart of a community is only as strong as first person plural—the names and faces of the "we" who work, live, play, and dream in that community. The growth of a community will only be positive as long as its people pass their defining values on to their children and newcomers.

That is what I hope to share with you in this space: the values of Keizer, reflected in the lives of the people who work, live, play, and dream here.

Defining Values:
Teachers, schools deserve thanks for impact on kids

This column was all but written when news came pouring out of Springfield, Oregon, on May 21st. After watching the news about the shootings at Thurston High School, my thoughts about schools and teachers were obviously affected by those images. Interestingly, most of what I had already written still rings true.

June 9th marks the end of an era for the Kirk family. An experience that began in September of 1988 with our oldest daughter, Sarah, will end with our youngest child, Matthew.

Sarah walked into a kindergarten class at Kennedy Elementary School in the fall of 1988 and was warmly greeted by Theresa Tartar-Strobel and June Sigleer. After a cheerful good-bye, I walked around the corner from the classroom and shed tears of anxiety. I was, after all, turning our firstborn child out into the world— a scary proposition for any parent.

I wondered what this change meant for our family, and would the trust that I needed to hand over to other adults be well placed? For the first time in her life, Sarah would be spending a good deal of her time in the company of strangers.

The last ten years have flown by. My memories are populated with many faces and names: Kim Grant, Nancy Montgomery, Rosemarie Jespersen, Joanne Crawford, Eleanor Hall, Nancy Lennon, Chris Patterson, and Bev Zwemke. Though not all, these were some of the teachers and staff that touched Sarah's life.

As a parent, I pondered the question: "Who will help give my child the ability to march to the beat of her own drum?" Mrs. Jespersen soared with Sarah when she had all of her multiplication facts memorized at the end of first grade. Mrs. Crawford, Mrs. Zwemke, and Mrs. Hall wrapped their arms around her and comforted her with words when she felt awkward or different. They reminded her, "You are an individual star meant to twinkle and shine in your very own way."

When Kaitlin went off to school, she found her exuberance and sense of humor celebrated and honored. Her teachers helped her realize that even though she might have the same red hair as her older sister, she was a person in her own right. I struggled with the thought: "What are the values of my child's village, and how will those values be communicated?" Kaitlin's teacher, Margie Guitierrez, and a rabbit named Trixie taught Kaitlin about independence and interdependence. Kaitlin developed a kind and caring attitude that was nurtured by example. Her teachers taught her lessons in life that aren't outlined in any educational curriculum.

Then Matthew's world expanded, and I wondered: "In this success-oriented culture, who will teach my child about the real meaning of success and failure?" Dan Burns, Scott Torgeson, Stephanie Miller, Deborah Ward, and Nanci Schneider may appear to be just names on a list. But Matthew can tell you a story about each of these wonderful people.

He can tell you how Mr. Burns taught him about magic and gaining self-confidence; Miss Ward used a violin to teach him some of the same lessons. Mr. Torgeson, or "Mr. T" to many of the children at Clear Lake Elementary, made Matthew laugh with stories about his dog. Mr. T's sense of humor helped Matthew to relax and realize that even adults aren't perfect. He learned that when you do silly things, it's OK to share laughter by telling tales on yourself.

When Matthew walks out of school on June 9, 1998, it will be the last day that John and I have a child in elementary school. I know that I'll have more than a few tears in my eyes when I go to say good-bye. And I will be having some of the same feelings of sorrow and loss that I felt on that September morning ten years ago.

In 1988 I didn't have the wisdom or foresight to know that my fears were unfounded. I didn't know that, like so many other giving teachers, Dixie Moravec was a part of our future. I couldn't know that she would become a friend, mentor, and partner in raising our children.

I realize now that "the end of an era" is really only another way of saying that a new beginning is about to happen. We're saying good-bye to grade school holiday programs, Jog-a-Thons, classroom parties, playground-scraped elbows and knees. But the memories will never fade, and the impression that all those teachers have had on Sarah, Kaitlin, Matthew, John, and me will never lose their impact.

When I walked into Howard Street Charter School last Wednesday and saw the way the staff was helping the students deal with the news out of Springfield, I realized, once again, the many ways that my children have been blessed by educators.

As we remember and pray for the families of Thurston High School, let's give thanks to Dixie, Scott, and all of the other teachers in this country. I dedicate this column, on the behalf of all parents. Let this be our "Parent Medal of Honor"—the highest form of gratitude that we can express—given to the men and women who help define the values in our children's lives each and every day.

Defining Values:
Limitations no match for strength of character

I've followed the stories about professional golfer Casey Martin with interest. The federal magistrate announced in February that Martin can play the top-level PGA and Nike tours with the aid of a golf cart. You may remember that Martin is the twenty-five-year-old from Eugene, Oregon, who suffers from a painful, genetic vascular problem of the leg. This problem prohibits him from walking the entire length of a golf course. The PGA Tour had sought to prevent Martin from using a golf cart because of its "walking only" rule. The PGA claimed this rule must be applied equally to all competitors.

On the day of the ruling, Martin stated, "I just want to be given a chance to play."

Martin's attorney, Martha Walters said, "We're seeking an equal opportunity for Mr. Martin to demonstrate his abilities."

In Keizer, Oregon, there is a young man who epitomizes everything Casey Martin stands for. Jake Stai is a fifteen-year-old freshman at McNary High School. An informal poll of his classmates at McNary tells a lot about Jake. (No, I'm not revealing my sources, Jake—so don't ask!) Jake is described as having a hilarious sense of humor, fun to be around, smart, kind, easy-to-be-with, and an all-around great guy.

I've had the privilege of knowing Jake since he was in the first grade, and I can understand why he is so well liked. Jake is one of those people who is so comfortable in his own skin that he is a joy to be around. The "beautiful people" in Hollywood, who so often suffer from identity crisis and spiritual neurosis, could learn a lesson from Jake.

I watched Jake help his brother Matthew practice shooting hoops at the "basketball court" outside my living room window one day. I marveled at his patience and wondered how many other teenage boys would choose to spend an afternoon with a third-grade brother—and all the while, appear to be having such a good time.

Jake's interest in music began when he was in kindergarten. That was the year that he submitted the following birthday wish list to his parents: a briefcase, a suit, a Bible, and piano lessons. Jake's mother, Karen, laughed heartily when she related this story to me.

"We weren't sure what the future held for a kindergartner with a wish list like that, but how could we complain," Karen told me.

Jake tried trombone lessons in the fifth grade but found that he just couldn't correctly get the technique for blowing the instrument and so stayed with piano. But when Jake was in the seventh grade and saw how much fun his older brother Brant was having doing marching band, Jake started taking lessons on the saxophone.

Jake is in the McNary Marching band and was sweating out the band camp last August. His mother told me "Jake's really concerned that he's not going to be able to get the hang of marching. It's possible that he might not be able to do marching band, but he's sure going to give it his best shot."

In December the band finished the end of an award-winning season with a celebration at the school. During the recognition ceremony, Jake was given awards for both the Most Improved Marcher and Most Inspirational Band Member. As I watched Jake walk up to get his awards, I had an insight into what makes Jake tick.

When I was in the fourth grade, a good friend of mine nominated her mother for "mother of the year." When Mrs. Biagi won, she was questioned about how being confined to a wheelchair with polio affected her ability to be a good mother. Even as a ten-year-old, I recognized the wisdom of her words.

Mrs. Biagi said, "We all have limitations of one kind or another. Some people have emotional, spiritual, or mental distress that can have a very crippling effect on their lives. My limitations just happen to be physical and therefore are a little more visible. But I've never let my limitations stop me from being all I can be."

By the way, Jake has cerebral palsy and has had to work hard at two tasks that most people take for granted: speaking and physical coordination. But Jake, like Mrs. Biagi and Casey Martin, has the hard-earned perception of knowing what it takes to be successful in life. John, Viscount Morley of Blackburn, wrote: "No man can climb out beyond the limitations of his own character." And Jake Stai, in a twist on those words, proves that the man with character can climb out beyond any limitations.

Defining Values:
Don't let a smoke screen hide that happy ending

They say a picture is worth a thousand words. So when I saw the billboard, with a picture and eight words, I tried to calculate the value of this ad concept. In my estimate, the Oregon Health Commission is getting its money's worth for its advertising dollars.

The ad was displayed high above River Road until recently. It showed a debonair gentleman with a cigarette in hand. He was asking, "Mind if I smoke?" His well-dressed woman companion answered, "Care if I die?" The billboard is part of the campaign funded by dollars from 1996's Ballot Measure 44. This measure increased cigarette taxes—10% of which is being used to fund antismoking activities.

I spoke with Gerry Odesio, the manager of the tobacco program at the State Health Division. She told me that several advertisement concepts were designed in California. California, Arizona, and Massachusetts also have funding available to use in educating the public about smoking.

"Rather than exhausting our money by spending the bulk of our funding on designing publicity, we chose to purchase the ads. We want to use funding so that the greatest amount of publicity can reach the largest number of people and impact them," Ms. Odesio said.

During some of my years employed "in the trenches of nursing," I wore the cap of an oncology nurse—a nurse who teaches, cares for, and provides support to cancer patients and their families. I have never smoked. But I am, I suppose, a bit like the reformed smoker who (having seen the light) has little tolerance for those who continue to smoke. On the other hand, I have enough understanding of addictive behavior to know that it isn't a matter of someone "just saying no" to smoking.

Education and a foundation for change are the two biggest keys to altering smoking behavior. People are not likely to give up an addictive behavior unless they recognize the negative consequences for themselves and their loved ones. It is often difficult, if not impossible, to make changes without the support needed to alter smoking habits.

I think what I like about the billboard is the immediate and "between the eyes" impact that it can make on readers. I know all the statistics on cancer deaths and health problems associated with smoking—so do most smokers. And we've all heard the arguments about people being entitled to individual liberties and having the right to abuse their own bodies, if they so choose. But this ad has a comeback for those arguments. It says, "What about the innocent bystander who will suffer the consequence of your smoking?"

I might have added one more line to the billboard. After the woman says, "Care if I die?" I'd have her continuing, "Because I care if *you* die!" That's a message that smokers, who sometimes are in denial or angry about the antismoking message, don't always hear.

I have an added incentive for wanting the antismoking message to be heard loud and clear: two teenage daughters and a son, Matthew, who turns 11 on May 13th. (Happy Birthday, Matthew!)

I've taken my own antismoking message into a local grocery store. Quentin is a young man who quit smoking several times while working at the store. During one of his "relapses," I spotted him in the parking lot with a cigarette in hand. I made sure that I got in his line that day. We joked back and forth, and I teased him that I could bring in pictures or slides of cancerous lungs or the kinds of needles that are used in giving chemotherapy.

The day before Quentin left for his enrollment in the military, he told me, "Well, I'll have to give it up for sure while I'm in boot camp!" We also talked about the high rate of smoking among military personnel.

Quentin has a sincere desire to quit smoking permanently. I like to think that some of my gentle chiding has helped him to realize other people care about his health, too. I think Quentin would be the first to agree with the Oregon Health Commission's campaign. He recognizes that the secondhand smoke he creates is not good for other adults or children, especially those with asthma or other respiratory ailments.

I picture Quentin home on military leave. He again realizes that he wants to quit smoking permanently. He checks out information about smoking cessation programs that is available through the American Cancer Society. He quits smoking—once and for all—and removes himself from the possibility of becoming a cancer smoking statistic.

I guess when the creative writer in me meets up with the registered nurse, I get a little carried away. But I've always loved a happy ending to a story. Like the other people in my community, I do care very much whether any person dies as a result of cigarette smoke. And, I personally, have seen far too many dreams go up in smoke.

Defining Values:
School charts new course for education, community

Charles Lindbergh was the first person to make a nonstop solo flight across the Atlantic Ocean in May 1927. Neil Armstrong was the first person to walk on the moon in July 1969. Move over, Charles and Neil. A 13-year-old young woman from Keizer and one of her female mentors have tested their wings this year and soared high above their lofty expectations.

At 4 foot, 10 inches tall, Amanda Ohrn hardly fits the profile of someone to fill the shoes of a Charles Lindbergh or a Neil Armstrong. And only time will tell if Amanda makes her way into any history books. But in her own way, Amanda helped break historical ground this year. Amanda was among the 13 graduating eighth graders at Howard Street Charter School on Monday, June 8th.

The Howard Street Charter School is the Salem-Keizer School District's first charter school. Charter schools are financed through the public school system, are held accountable for the same educational requirements and standards, and must comply with state and federal law. But they have the freedom—and challenge—to meet those requirements by creating a unique school culture that incorporates the needs and desires of the communities that they serve.

Howard Street School was founded on the slogan, "Preparing Children to Live in the World." The theme of "Einstein, Ellington, and Esperanto" indicates the emphasis that is placed on science and math, the fine arts, and proficiency in languages. The challenge to staff is to take the 75% per-student operating funds from the district and make these goals a reality. (The remaining 25% of funding is held by the district and utilized for the school's administrative costs.)

As the mother of a seventh-grade student enrolled at the school, I can tell you that the 102 students completing their first year epitomize how the school has met those goals. The principal and her fine staff have given those students the tools they need to succeed. Whenever I walked into the building, I saw students who were excited about learning, who collaborated with one another and staff, and who were respectful of others.

If you want another perspective, just talk to Amanda Ohrn. She'll tell you that, even though she was glad to be accepted into the school, she also was a little apprehensive. She joined 104 students from around the district who came together last September in an effort to create a new middle school community. That might have been a tough choice for Amanda to make—especially when all of her efforts would produce a school that she could call "home" for only one year. But Amanda wanted to go to a smaller school and to be part of an environment where she was challenged and appreciated for the gifts she has to offer. So, in spite of knowing only one other student who had enrolled at Howard Street, Amanda took the plunge into the unknown.

Joni Gilles is another Keizer resident who took the plunge right along with Amanda. She is a longtime educator, and former McNary High School teacher, who left a position at Regis High School to become the principal and guiding force at the new charter school. She might not have anticipated the 16-hour days and manic juggling act that she was about to take on. But Mrs. Gilles walked into the wing of the old Leslie building (which houses her students) with a smile on her face. That smile, along with her contagious excitement, continues to lead the way. She defined her goals last September as creating a school where people are listened to, involvement is welcome, and students give back to the community.

You don't have to look any further than Amanda to know that Mrs. Gilles has met those goals. Amanda told me last Friday, "One of the best things about my school is that I know everyone here and they know me. My teachers really know who I am!"

Amanda's teachers know that she is a gifted viola player who picked up a viola only five months ago and that she will delight you with her music. They know that Amanda excels at Japanese and in the Honors Geometry class that she completed at South Salem High School. Her teachers will tell you that she is a caring student who has played an important role in shaping her community, both inside and outside the walls of the school.

Amanda will be testing her wings again next year when she starts as a freshman in South Salem High School's International Baccalaureate program. Mrs. Gilles will return to a new set of challenges and goals as Howard Street Charter School begins its second year of operation. When you see Amanda or Joni Gilles, be sure that you offer them words of congratulations. They may only be making "one small step for womankind," but their dreams and aspirations are creating blue skies in the future of education.

Defining Values:
If you can't take a joke . . .

Humor is a terrible thing to waste. It turns frown lines into laugh lines. It changes the bumps in the road of life into an opportunity to giggle at an unplanned, and newly discovered, amusement ride. It provides the inspiration for some of the best tip jar slogans around. It has the ability to turn shrieks of pain into chortles of laughter. It's the glue that holds our lives together when we otherwise think we might fall apart.

Fortunately for me, I live in Keizer amongst a city of people who seem to have the same ability to laugh at life and themselves that I do; we don't get even—we find a way to laugh.

Stephanie Rogerson is a delightful and typical four-year-old. When my daughters, Sarah and Kaitlin, baby-sat Stephanie at our house recently, we knew we were in for an amusing time (in a stream-of-consciousness kind of way).

Shortly after her arrival, Stephanie announced, "I'll be the mother; I'm Meg. Sarah, you'll be the daughter; you're Emily." Apparently, one of Stephanie's favorite games is choosing other names for herself and the people around her. While this is a fun game for a four-year-old, for those of us older folks (who may be a little memory-impaired) this can be a little stressful. Whenever I slipped and called one of the girls by her real name, Stephanie would adamantly correct me.

"No, I'm Meg! She's Emily!"

We decided that this kind of play could precipitate a real identity crisis for Stephanie's mother, Christine. I envisioned Christine wandering around their home with a dazed look on her face, muttering, "Let's see, I'm Lola and you're Pulooza. No, that's not right. You're Tarzan and I'm Jane. Now, I know I can get this right . . . who am I today?"

At one point, Stephanie asked what new name she should call me. Sarah, trying to be helpful, suggested, "We call her Marmie as a nickname sometimes. So you could call her Marmie, too."

"No, I'll call her Barbie," Stephanie responded.

Thinking about the spontaneous and uninhibited humor of a four-year-old automatically makes me think of Don Vowell. Of course, if you happen to know Don, or have ever spent five minutes in his company, you know that this is an accurate description of what makes Don so charming.

I have learned to never approach a conversation with Don when I urgently need to visit the bathroom, or at least not in a social situation where there isn't a mop readily handy. That's the kind of reaction that Don produces whenever he has the chance to verbally play with words and bring a smile to your face.

The readers of the *Keizertimes* know that Don ran a hilarious campaign for mayor last year. He cornered people in the grocery store to cajole them with his wit and try to talk them into voting for him. He badgered Les Zaitz until Les finally relented and allowed Don guest editorial space to announce his candidacy.

Now I understand that he is trying to talk my fifteen-year-old daughter into being his campaign manager. (Ask Don about his new "Vowell Movement" campaign slogan. OK, Don, here's the plug I promised you—now where's my five bucks!) Come to think of it, maybe Don is the perfect candidate for mayor. If he can just get the folks with the "laughter platform" to endorse him, we can all breath a little easier when he is occupied at city hall and off of the streets of Keizer.

I've had more encounters in the last few months with laughter than I care to confess. Those of you who make your living working with a word processor know exactly what I mean. Whenever I have a particularly enlightening train of thought going, my nimble fingers manage to hit the wrong keys. Then I'm immediately blinded by either red or green <u>underlines</u> pointing out my mistakes to me. (Thanks a lot, Bill Gates and Microsoft!)

This wouldn't be so bad, except that when I try to spell check, my computer has such absurd recommendations that I find myself laughing more than writing. The first time I typed Kathy Kirk, one of the suggestions that popped up for "Kirk" was "quirk."

Only this morning, I typed the header to my column and glanced up to see *"Defoaming Values"* staring me in the face. (I filed that title in the back of my head for future reference. I can see the article I'll write. Read "Defoaming Values." This is the incredible story of the industrial chemicals that are used, and the brave custodians who use them, to clean the rooms after unsavory right-wing groups meet.)

And then there is grammar check. I have yet to convince my computer that I like writing long sentences and to heck with what "The Elements of Style" has to say about run-on sentences!

Recently I heard, through Nancy Vowell, that Don was complaining about his election coverage. Don has never had his picture displayed with any of his guest opinions. Knowing full well what kind of comeback to expect, I approached Don. I said, "You know, Don, Les Zaitz told me he only publishes the pictures of young and good-looking people in the *Keizertimes*."

Don replied deadpan, "That's my point. What is your picture doing in the paper?"

Now, I don't mind playing straight man once in a while, as long as it produces a good laugh. But I'm also very insistent that you keep my name straight. You can call me "Marmie," but don't call me "Barbie"!

Defining Values:
Exchange blends cultures, one visit at a time

An estimated 140,000 people died as a result of the atom bomb that fell on Hiroshima on August 6, 1945. 70,000 more died at Nagasaki. These numbers are staggering and incomprehensible. And behind every number is the face of a person, the contours of which may be different than yours or mine—but a human being whose history ended with those bombings.

My family greeted Satomi Ohashi and Hatsue Sato 53 years and 1 day after the beginning of the nuclear age. These exchange students came as weekend guests. Tokyo International University of America places Japanese students in American homes. TIUA's brochure explains, "The underlying philosophy of the Tomodachi Program is that the fabric of our culture is woven within the family." "Tomodachi" is Japanese for "friend."

Satomi and Hatsue are students from Kyoei Gakuen Junior College in Tokyo. They both live at home with their parents and one younger brother, but that's where the similarities stop and their individual personalities take over. Satomi is quiet and demure. In fact, she wrote that she wanted her host family to know, "I am very shy." At first, she was more comfortable letting Hatsue be the spokesperson. Hatsue, on the other hand, demonstrated an outgoing personality from the start. As we were leaving TIUA, she fluttered her hand against her shirt to demonstrate a racing heart and said, "I am nervous about going!" But she spoke with such gusto that we knew she was an explorer who wasn't about to miss anything!

My family hosted a student for 3 weeks last summer, and both Sarah and Kaitlin speak a smattering of Japanese. We had such a wonderful time that we felt more excited than apprehensive this year. Plus we were armed with the information that Satomi and Hatsue favor hamburgers and French fries—a sure sign that these girls were going to bond with the Kirk clan!

So, for 48 hours we became a family of seven. We went to John's company picnic at Silver Creek Falls. We had dinner at a Mount Angel restaurant. We rented an English version of a Japanese animated film and all laughed in the same language. The girls were interested in sports, so my daughters organized a basketball game at Clear Lake, then moved on to play tennis at McNary High.

Satomi responded with typical teenage enthusiasm when Sarah offered to paint her fingernails. Hatsue opted for a game of Nintendo with Matthew. Our family room filled with the typical noise, smells, and action of a Sunday afternoon at home.

Throughout our visit, we traded questions about our countries and cultures. We talked about the memories that Hatsue and Satomi would take home. Hatsue was surprised by the many cars and the big American houses.

When I teased and asked if she wanted to take Matthew home, she replied, "My house is too narrow," and she agreed that "one brother is enough!" When I asked Hatsue what her parents thought about the United States, her perhaps not so surprising answer was, "They are afraid of America and Americans. They are afraid of the guns in America."

At the end of our visit, we invited Hatsue and Satomi to come to a barbecue later in the week. Perhaps 48 hours isn't enough time to dispel the fears created by atomic bombs and international television images. But, like the people at TIUA, I'm hoping my family and I helped create another image. We hope the fabric of our future is woven in a culture that celebrates and values the human family—different contours and all.

Defining Values:
Team values players with heart

If you didn't see the last two games on June 28th, you've missed your chance to see some of the best baseball action around. But as they say in the baseball trade, just "Wait until next year!"

No, I'm not talking about watching the Volcanoes or catching an All-Star game at the Keizer field. I had the privilege of watching the Willow Lake Nursery team play their final game in this season's Challenger League. I left with a clear understanding of true sportsmanship thanks to team members Blake McCracken, Molly Blake, Erik and Matthew Morgan, Forrest Gauthier, Erin Richards, Louie Schuster, K. C. Gale, Rachel Lehman, Eric Grimm, Staci Raleigh, Lindley and Jessica Ferguson, and their coaches, Dale Grimm and Ron Raleigh. Their enthusiasm turned a dull Sunday afternoon into a powerful lesson about the joys of recreational sports and friendship.

Challenger leagues were developed nationally in 1988. The Salem/Keizer/Silverton League was created 8 years ago to provide opportunities for anyone, ages 6 through 20, not able to participate on a regular baseball team. Karen Wren launched the effort for a team. Kim Josted, who was looking for a team for her son, Chase, coordinated the administrative efforts. Mary Lynn Morgan soon joined them.

Challenger league games are "played loosely" like regulation ball games, with some notable exceptions. No score is kept, an inning consists of a team rotating through the batting order, and batters are allowed to swing until they make contact or use a tee to hit from if they so choose. Players can have a buddy on the field if they need assistance. For instance, wheelchair-bound members can have a buddy push them around the bases and help them retrieve balls that they can't reach.

Play is rotated on fields throughout Salem, Keizer, and Silverton. One or two games are played each week, usually on Tuesday evenings and Sunday afternoons. Some teams may practice, but most don't once the six-week season begins. A game consists of two to four innings depending on the weather and interest level of the players.

Mary Lynn is a kindergarten teacher at Cummings Elementary School, and her sons, Erik and Matthew, have participated on a team every year of the league's existence. Mary Lynn explained that the teams provide youngsters with physical and developmental disabilities the chance to experience fun and camaraderie. "Our teams are what all Little League teams should be," she said.

If you don't know which parent belongs to which child, you won't find out by listening to the spectators cheering throughout the game. I heard Sue Nelson, a teacher and former team coach, as she praised Tim Wirch's hit with, "Good hit, Tim!" An instant later she called, "Good catch, Blake!"

In fact, the kids are considerate of one another regardless of their team jersey. As I watched players being supportive of one another, Mary Lynn related a story about Erik. Once Erik fielded a ball and then tagged a hearing-impaired player named Raven. Erik jumped up and down shouting, "Hurray!" for all of 30 seconds. Then, not wanting to hurt her feelings, he turned to Raven and signed, "Sorry."

Because the children come from a number of schools and locations, teams were originally established by placing kids who knew one another together. Many have returned on a yearly basis, and bonds have grown between the players and their families. Some kids tire of the activity, take off a year or two, and then come back. Others lose interest or move to a regular ball team. But there are always plenty of youngsters waiting in the wings.

Only resources available limit the number of teams in the league. Lenora and John Blake have sponsored the Willow Lake Nursery team since the league's inception. The three other returning sponsors this year included Huston Sport Photography, Abiqua Optimist, and Silverton Elks. A $20 enrollment fee is used to help cover expenses, but scholarships are available to any child who requests one. The league has had as many as six teams, and Mary Lynn stated, "Obviously the more sponsors we have, the more kids it allows to play."

Sign-ups for the 1999 season won't occur until next spring. But you can bet that Blake McCracken will spend the rest of this year relishing his center field line drive. And though Forrest Gauthier arrived late to the last game, he will remember the hero's welcome he received. As he ran into his dugout, his teammates hugged him and shouted, "All right, Forrest is here!"

If you can't wait until next year to get involved with this wonderful league, call Mary Lynn Morgan. They are always looking for sponsors, coaches, and helpers of all ages. And, in this league, a player with heart will always be valued as a team member!

Defining Values:
A tribute to working moms

Erma Bombeck and I have shared a strange sisterhood of souls since I was eleven years old. I "met" Erma through a Sacramento newspaper that I was reading while visiting my grandmother. The column was about a trip that Erma and her husband made to the emergency room with their young son after he had devoured a tube of blue paint.

I remarked to my grandmother, "The woman who writes this column is cynical and deranged. I'm glad she's not my mother."

My grandmother, who was a licensed practical nurse, explained the meaning of satire to me and assured me that Erma Bombeck was a very funny lady. I reread the column and had a belly laugh.

More than a few years have passed since that day. Erma's voice has woven in and out of my life, sustaining me with her wit and wisdom, and shaping me with her poignant observations about women and our place in the world.

I read Erma's columns sporadically throughout my youth and early twenties. A column she wrote in 1976 was about women like Margaret Mitchell, who wrote "Gone With the Wind" at age 37, and Golda Meir, who was elected prime minister of Israel at age 76. And it was about Erma Bombeck who, at the age of 37, "Sat at her kitchen window year after year and watched everyone else do it and then said to herself, 'It's my turn.'" I found the column interesting, but I was busy dreaming how to complete my education as a nurse.

I graduated from nursing school in May 1980, the same month that Erma published a column about the mothers of disabled children. As a registered nurse, the truth of her moving words touched me, even though I didn't yet have any experience as a mother.

When I became a mother for the first time in 1982, I reread many of Erma's previous columns that had seemed interesting in passing but suddenly were a gold mine of the feelings that I was now experiencing. Her column published in 1980 summed it up for me: "I brought children into this lousy, mixed-up world because when you love someone and they love you back, the world doesn't look that lousy or seem that mixed up."

By 1987, I was the mother of three children—all under the age of four and a half. "Aunt Erma's" old columns kept me laughing and sane. Her self-described flippant approach to motherhood was the best reminder of what she wrote: ". . . he who laughs . . . lasts!"

There were days when I wasn't sure if the screams I heard were an angry baby and toddlers—or voices in my head. I would find comfort in those screams, though, when I read her words. She described what it would be like someday when the kids were gone: "Only a voice crying, 'Why don't you grow up?' and the silence echoing, 'I did.'"

On April 22, 1996, Erma Bombeck died of a chronic disease. She had been struggling with medical problems for a number of years. Again our lives seemed to be interwoven. I worked part-time as an oncology nurse for many years. In her book "I Want to Grow Hair, I Want to Grow Up, I Want to Go to Boise" she wrote about the heroics of kids surviving cancer. I worked mostly with adult cancer patients but had seen firsthand the tragedies and triumphs that her book exposed.

In January of 1998 I faced a crossroads of another sort. I sat at my kitchen window and wondered if, at age 44, I could leave the world of nursing behind and prosper as a writer. I reflected on Erma's column from 1976. I recalled that Erma Bombeck was only 5 foot, 2 inches tall ($\frac{1}{4}$ inch taller than I am). I decided that I had looked up to her for too long to ignore her advice now.

I was at a gathering of women in my neighborhood recently. Some of the women are full-time at-home moms, some collect a full-time paycheck, and others, like myself, fall somewhere in between. I've read about the "mommy wars"—women taking opposite stances and not having anything in common depending on their employment status. But I looked around and marveled at the wonderful camaraderie that was taking place.

Erma Bombeck was born in a different time and generation than any of the women in this group. In fact, some of these women are of a different generation than me. But Erma left a legacy that is a clue to the joy we find in each other's company.

Erma hit the nail on the head: All mothers are working women. Erma pointed out long ago that the bonds we share—from the trivial, dirty socks and litter boxes, to the poignant, hurt feelings and broken dreams—are tighter than any issues created by a pay stub. I have a strong sense that Erma looked down from heaven on our coffee klatch that day and smiled through her tears.

Defining Values:
Examples abound for kids

I've given my children the same "don't take rides with strangers" lecture that every mother in every town recites. I've tried to help them establish criteria for good judgment. But trying to distill "how you'll know when it's safe to rely on other people" into words is a tough task. How do I teach them the difference between taking a risk and having faith? I'm fortunate. I live in a community where people value your word and give you the benefit of the doubt.

Randy Stoltz is one of my favorite clerks at a local grocery store. Over the years, we've exchanged stories about our children's trials, tribulations, and successes. I've learned enough about Randy to know that, aside from being an accurate checker, he's kind, caring, and considerate.

Randy has checked and bagged a lot of groceries for me, so what happened the other day shouldn't have surprised me. After keying in the wrong produce code, he was correcting the price of my lettuce. I told him that I was particularly watchful of prices since, only the week before, another checker had overcharged me two dollars by hitting the wrong code.

"I only discovered the mistake after I got home, and I never did get around to bringing my receipt back in," I complained.

"Well, I'll just fix that right now," Randy replied as he proceeded to credit my current receipt with two dollars.

When I was reflecting on this incident, I was reminded of a story that a friend related. Nedora Counts went into a local feed store where she occasionally shops and where she always receives exceptional customer service. She was trying to make up her mind about buying a cinch and wanted to know if she could exchange it and get her money back, if she changed her mind.

"Why don't you take it with you and see if it works for the horse you have in mind? If so, you can pay for it the next time you come in, or else bring it back then," she was told.

Then Nedora asked if she needed to sign something to show that she was taking the merchandise without paying for it. She was a bit taken aback when she was told, "No, no need to do that. Just let us know whether you decide to keep it or not."

Shopping trips have an interesting way of providing lessons. One time I pushed a cart full of groceries to my car only to discover that I had locked my keys inside. I went back into the store and asked if I could keep my groceries in the cooler. I explained what I had done, and that I was on my way to meet my husband, John, at the Keizer Little League Fields where he was coaching our son, Matthew, in a soccer game.

"I'll walk up and watch the game. Afterwards, I'll catch a ride back with John and unlock the car. Then I'll collect my groceries," I told the clerk.

As my groceries were being taken to the cooler, a woman, who had just finished buying groceries, stopped me. "You'll be late for your son's soccer game if you walk; let me take you since it really won't be that far out of my way," she insisted. And contrary to what both of our mothers had taught us, she provided the ride that made me feel good for the rest of the day. She offered, and I accepted, a simple act of kindness.

In Robert Frost's beautiful poem "Bravado," he writes about walking and looking cautiously up at the very stars that "might not have missed me when they shot and fell." Fortunately for those of us who love poetry, Robert Frost knew the truth about balancing the need for safety with the faith needed for personal growth.

And like the people of Keizer, he knew, "It was a risk I had to take—and took." Here in Keizer, my children have living examples—people to show them how to read circumstances, how to choose the higher road of trust when suspicion has become such a normal part of everyday life.

Defining Values:
Cell towers cast shadow from east coast to west

In the first half of the twentieth century, universal service was the goal of the telephone industry in the United States. Every household was to own a telephone. After reading articles in several issues of the March *Washington Post* newspaper, I shudder to think what the telephone industry has in mind for the twenty-first century.

According to the *Post,* Bell Atlantic Mobile has requested approval to place cell phone towers in Rock Creek Park in Washington, D.C. Bell Atlantic claims that more than 3,000 calls a month are interrupted because of poor reception in the park. Before you conclude that these facts have no bearing on the life of Oregonians, perhaps I should tell you a little more about Rock Creek Park.

You should know that Rock Creek Park is a *national* park that has been virtually unchanged since its creation in 1890. One reader of the *Post* compared Bell's proposal with the idea of opening a McDonald's in Yosemite National Park so that visitors would have the convenience of buying food whenever hunger hits them.

Another D.C. resident, who wrote in protest of Bell's proposal, stated, "Rock Creek Park is one of the Washington area's treasures. We must not allow commercial interests that are disguised as customer service to ravage a magnificent landscape."

I spoke with Cindy Cox, Assistant Superintendent of Rock Creek Park, recently. She told me that Bell Atlantic's completed application for cell phone towers was accepted on May 13, 1998. The National Park Service will take 60 days to review the application. Using guidelines and information from a number of sources, including the National Environmental Policy Act, a determination will be made. The application can be approved or denied. Or it can be held for further evaluation until a final determination is made.

I calculated that, living in Keizer, we live approximately 2,330 miles from the park. (This would be by crow's flight, not calculated in microwaves via cellular telephone.) The people at the *Washington Post* may not have any interest in my opinion. But since it is also my national park, I offer a perspective that perhaps some people can understand.

Recently, I returned from fifth grade "outdoor school." I traveled on a gravel logging road at ten o'clock at night, and have to admit that the cell telephone in my glove compartment gave me an added sense of security.

But I have a couple of practical suggestions for the people at Bell Atlantic Mobile. According to the *Post* article, there are pay phones located throughout the park, and there are alternate routes around the park where continuous cellular transmission is possible. I would suggest using these alternatives to erecting cell phone towers.

When I worked as a home health and home infusion nurse for approximately 5 years, I traveled extensively throughout the Willamette Valley. So I can certainly understand all of the practical and professional reasons for needing to use cellular telephones. I would suggest that the people in Washington, D.C., adopt the more "rugged individual" attitude that I have developed as an Oregon adoptee.

The entire time that I worked in the home care nursing field, I never traveled with a cell phone. I carried a mobile pager through which my company and my family could reach me. I carried a purse full of change, and I knew the location of virtually every pay phone that exists along the routes that I traveled to patients' homes.

I have fond memories of being paged on Peoria Road near Corvallis and wondering, "Now, how far back was that convenience store and gas station?" I also have fond memories of paying particular attention to which pay phones actually provided some kind of shelter for making a call in the middle of an unusually wet February.

Though I may relate those "fond" memories with tongue in cheek, I am happy to say that I never encountered an emergency or other situation with which I was unable to deal—in spite of the fact that I wasn't packing a cellular telephone. And it feels good to know that my chosen line of work was not responsible for causing another cell phone tower to be erected in the Willamette Valley.

I think the people of Keizer value and appreciate the use of modern conveniences as much as the people in Washington, D.C. I also think we value a lifestyle that puts pristine, natural beauty higher up on our list of priorities than convenience and inflated self-importance.

Defining Values:
Some heroes do more than hit the ball

Gary Gaetti, the Cubs third baseman, got a bone-crunching hug after Mark McGwire's record-breaking 62nd home run. He said of McGwire, "The guy doesn't know his own strength." Like Mark McGwire, my friend Glenn is a big man. Glenn's also a strong man, and, fortunately for him, he *does* know his own strength.

A multitude of sportscasters has followed McGwire's attempt to break the home run record set by Roger Maris in 1961. In some ways, this coverage has been typical of the media blitz that surrounds any major sports event. But I've also been pleased to discover that McGwire, like Roger Maris, seems to have the ability to put this historical event into perspective.

When Maris set the home run record 37 years ago, my friend Glenn was just a young child. Last spring when McGwire was dreaming about assaulting the home run record, Glenn had already begun his own battle. In November 1997, Glenn was diagnosed with multiple myeloma, a cancer of the bone marrow. His life since then has been filled with days of chemotherapy, blood tests, and fighting infections.

Mark McGwire has a life outside the limelight of the baseball stadium. When he hit the record-tying home run, one of his biggest joys was having his ten-year-old son there to witness the event. He described his actions after the hit, "Next thing I know I saw him at home plate. I gave him a hug and a kiss and told him I loved him. What a wonderful feeling a father could have."

Glenn knows that feeling too. He has a whole other life outside of the cancer clinic. He has a full-time job, a loving wife and two sons, and many friends. As Glenn fights his disease, he continues to live his life like he always has—a hard-working, generous, and outgoing man.

He makes time to visit and offer encouragement to other patients. He trades recipes and some of his gourmet cooking secrets. He organizes his time to spend it with the people who mean the most to him. Glenn deals with his cancer like he has faced the four open-heart surgeries that his youngest son has undergone. Glenn draws his strength from his earthly family and from the renewal he says he finds from his Father above.

The Maris family played prominently in McGwire's quest to break the home run record. They sat in the baseball stands and relived memories of Roger Maris. Rich Maris, looking the spitting image of his famous father, hugged McGwire after the record-breaking home run.

A close family friend revealed several tidbits about the events after Roger Maris set his own record. He disclosed that when a reporter asked Maris what he hit, meaning the kind of pitch, Maris replied, "I hit a baseball." And after a long evening, Maris stopped into a church across from the restaurant where he ate dinner so that he could attend midnight mass.

It's been fun to follow the excitement generated around baseball lately. Mark McGwire broke a long-standing record while demonstrating sportsmanship and behavior that we all hope our children will emulate. McGwire and the Maris family also helped remind us of the importance of our connections and our relationships to one another.

But in the plain light of everyday life, it seems pretty obvious that what Mark McGwire hit was indeed simply a baseball. If I'm going to grant "hero status" to anyone, I'll probably reserve it for my friend Glenn and his wife, Karla. They already know the score and could pass a few tips to Mark McGwire and the rest of us about loving and valuing the people in our lives.

Bibliography

Brooks, B. S., Kennedy, G., Moen, D. R., & Ranly, D. (1999). *News reporting and writing* (6th ed.). Boston: Bedford/St. Martin's.

Calkins, L. M. (1986). *The art of teaching writing.* Portsmouth, NH: Heinemann.

Calkins, L. M. (1994). *The art of teaching writing* (New ed.). Portsmouth, NH: Heinemann.

Corbett, E. (1973). *The little English handbook: Choices and conventions.* New York: John Wiley.

Dahl, R. (1982). *The BFG.* New York: Knopf.

Fowler, H. R. (1980). *The Little, Brown handbook.* Boston: Little, Brown.

Goldstein, N. (Ed.). (1998). *The Associated Press stylebook and libel manual.* Reading, MA: Addison-Wesley.

Hale, G. (Ed.). (1996). *Classic clip art: Thousands of copyright-free images.* New York: Glorya Hale Books/Random House Value.

Hoban, R. (1968). *A birthday for Frances.* New York: Scholastic Book Services.

Holiday spot illustrations: 94 copyright-free designs. (1996). Toronto, Ontario, Canada: Dover.

Kirk, Kathy (1998-1999). Defining values [Selected weekly newspaper columns]. *Keizertimes.* (Keizer, OR)

Kirk, Kaitlin (1999). Flower child. In *A celebration of the Northwest's young poets.* Smithfield, UT: Creative Communications.

Lovell, J., & Kluger, J. (1994). *Apollo 13.* New York: Simon & Schuster/Pocket Books. (Previously titled *Lost Moon*)

Park, B. (1995). *Mick Harte was here.* New York: Random House.

Rowling, J. K. (1997). *Harry Potter and the sorcerer's stone.* New York: Scholastic.

Rowling, J. K. (1999a). *Harry Potter and the chamber of secrets.* New York: Scholastic.

Rowling, J. K. (1999b). *Harry Potter and the prisoner of Azkaban.* New York: Scholastic.

Silverstein, S. (1974a). *A light in the attic.* New York: Harper & Row.

Silverstein, S. (1974b). *Where the sidewalk ends.* New York: Harper & Row.

Spandel, V. (1996). *Seeing with new eyes.* Portland, OR: Northwest Regional Educational Laboratory.

Strunk, W., Jr., & White, E. B. (1959). *The elements of style.* New York: Macmillan.

Viorst, J. (1972). *Alexander and the terrible, horrible, no good, very bad day.* New York: Scholastic.

White, E. B. (1952). *Charlotte's web.* New York: Harper & Row.

Writing assessment and evaluation. (1996). Salem, OR: Oregon Department of Education.

Index

Adjectives, 40, 46
Alexander and the Terrible, Horrible, No Good, Very Bad Day, 12

"Baby Blues," 15
Beginning. *See* Story beginning
BFG, The, 12
Birthday for Francis, A, 13
Brainstorming:
    for details that match main ideas, 25, 67
    for ideas and topics, 65, 68, 108

Charlotte's Web, 13, 94
Children:
    as storytellers, 1
Conclusion. *See* Story conclusion
Content:
    focusing on, 38
    matching newspaper parts to, 35
Conventions, writing. *See* Writing conventions

Dahl, Roald, 12
Descriptive words, 22
Descriptive writing, 18, 32
Details, 65
    brainstorming to match main ideas, 25
    communicating main idea with, 20
    eliminating, 20
    focusing on, 86
    matching with main ideas, 24, 65
    organizing, 65
    sorting pictures to focus on, 21
    sorting words to match with main ideas, 26
    using drawings to examine, 22
    using facts for, 20
    using memory for, 20
    using senses for, 20
Dialects, 52
Dictionaries, checking spelling with, 99-100
Drawings:
    creating to focus on main ideas, 23
    using to examine details, 22

Expository writing, 18, 31

"Family Circus, The," 14, 15
Final draft, proofreading and editing, 106-107
"Flower Child," 57
Fluency, 58
    changing sentences to create, 64
Fluent sentences, 55
    joining sentence fragments to create, 61
    selecting, 62
    writing, 62
Fluent sentence structure, 59
Fluent writing techniques, 63

Hoban, Russell, 13

Ideas. *See* Main ideas
Idea webs:
    for focusing a topic, 67, 68
Imaginative writing, 18, 32-33

Keane, Bil, 14
Kirk, Kaitlin, 57
Kirk, Kathy, 58, 109
Kirkman, Rick, 15

Leads, 76
    purpose of, 77
    writing "reader-catching," 77-78
    See also Story beginning
Literary characters:
    exploring to express voice, 12-13
Lovell, Jim, 18

Made-up words, 59